The New Western W

Martin Shaw

The New Western Way of War

Risk-Transfer War and its Crisis in Iraq

Martin Shaw

polity

First published in 2005 by Polity Press

Polity Press
65 Bridge Street
Cambridge CB2 1UR, UK

Polity Press
350 Main Street
Malden, MA 02148, USA

ISBN: 0-7456-3410-9
ISBN: 0-7456-3411-7(pb)

A catalogue record for this book is available from the British Library.

Typeset in 10 on 12 pt Berling
by SNP Best-set Typesetter Ltd., Hong Kong
Printed and bound in Great Britain by MPG Books, Bodmin,
Cornwall.

The publisher has used its best endeavours to ensure that the URLs
for external websites referred to in this book are correct and active at
the time of going to press. However, the publisher has no responsibility for the websites and can make no guarantee that a site will remain
live or that the content is or will remain appropriate.

Every effort has been made to trace all copyright holders, but if any
have been inadvertently overlooked the publishers will be pleased to
include any necessary credits in any subsequent reprint or edition.

For further information on Polity, visit our website: www.polity.co.uk

Contents

Tables

Acknowledgements

I first developed the idea of 'risk-transfer war' to explain the disparity between military and civilian casualties in the first phase of the Global War on Terror in Afghanistan. I discussed it with my final-year and master's students in war and peace studies at Sussex, and later in seminars in various universities, and I was helped by the responses of many who took part in the discussions. The first full presentation of the argument was 'Risk-Transfer Militarism, Small Massacres and the Historic Legitimacy of War', in *International Relations*, 16, 3, 2002, pp. 343–60. I am grateful to the then editor, Michael Cox, for quickly publishing this article, and to Sage Publishers for allowing me to use it in subsequent work. During late 2003, I developed some of the theoretical basis and applied the ideas to what was happening in Iraq, with the support of a research grant from the Centro Militare di Studi Strategici, Rome. I owe special thanks to the head of the centre's Military Sociology department, Alessandro Gobbicchi, for his encouragement. This research has informed chapter 5. Finally, the time to write this book in the first half of 2004 was provided by a research fellowship on 'Understanding Violence against Civilians: Genocide and Risk-Transfer War', awarded by the Economic and Social Research Council. I am very grateful to the council for its support. Later, my colleagues Julian Reid and Stefan Elbe provided invaluable comments on the typescript.

As always, my biggest debt is to my family, above all Annabel, for their support.

Martin Shaw, Brighton, May 2004

Introduction

In the early twenty-first century most Western political leaders and thinkers continue to believe that they may use war justly and efficiently as a means of political action. They sometimes disagree about particular decisions: many dissented from the US and British invasion of Iraq in 2003. But they agree on the general principle: blowing people up – for this is what war mostly means today – remains a legitimate, even if regrettable, way of achieving political goals. Of course, the people they aim to blow up are those who have taken up arms for hostile and disreputable political causes. They do not intend to blow up civilians or non-combatants. That, if it happens, is by definition 'accidental'. But above all, in blowing up as many enemies and as few civilians as necessary, they aim to avoid many of their own soldiers or aircrew getting killed. Indeed, if averting risk to military personnel means increasing the risk of civilians being killed or harmed, then that unfortunately is a price that civilians must pay.

What I have just described, and what this book is about, is a central aspect of how the West currently fights its wars. I call it *risk-transfer war* because it centres on minimizing life-risks to the military – and hence all-important political and electoral risks to their masters – at the expense not only of 'enemies' but also of those whom the West agrees are 'innocent'. It is a way of fighting war that has been perfected over the last twenty-five years, in the shadow of the disastrous US war in Vietnam, in the Falklands-Malvinas, Gulf, Kosovo and Afghan wars, as well as in various lesser 'interventions', before the most recent campaign in Iraq.

The advocates of new Western warfare make much of its 'precision' weaponry and sophisticated computerized systems of command and control. Critics make a lot of how media are controlled to stop Western citizens seeing whom their militaries are blowing up. Both are partially right, but there is much more to it than either of these perceptions. This book explores the core of the new way of war by setting out (in the central chapter 4) fifteen key 'rules' according to which it operates.

The three chapters before that lay the foundations for this account of its rules. Chapter 1 outlines the *history* of the new Western way, showing how it has developed over a series of wars in the last quarter-century. Chapter 2 gives a critical outline of the existing *theories* of ways of war in general and the new Western way in particular, to show how others have grasped their main features and to suggest the issues that arise. Chapter 3 outlines the *framework* of contemporary warfare as a whole, suggesting that the Western 'risk-transfer' way of war is one variant of the general 'global surveillance' mode of warfare, competing with other ways of war used by other armed actors.

The chapters after the 'rules' have rather different roles. Chapter 5 takes the Iraq War as the most recent and ambitious example of a new Western campaign. It analyses the war as an *economy of risk*: the ways that political risks and life-risks have been imagined, and how different groups have been exposed to and experienced them, have shaped the practice and outcomes of the war. I argue that Iraq has been a case of serious risk rebound, as insurgency, terrorism and the thinness of the manifest case for war have combined to push up the human and political cost of the war for the USA.

In chapter 6, I take this argument further, to suggest that the failure in Iraq represents a *crisis* of the whole new way of war that has been developed since Vietnam. The Bush administration, with its ill-conceived Global War on Terrorism, has broken some of the cardinal 'rules' of the new Western way of war, and has invited the risk rebound that it has suffered. However, this failure has also brought into question the very foundation of contemporary Western warfighting: the idea that war can be a precise, clinical, spatially and temporally *discrete* affair without fundamental ramifications for society and politics in the West.

This book is a work of social theory and analysis that tries to capture fast-moving political and military realities. However, it also presents a moral and political argument. At the beginning of the twenty-first century, the West is at a crossroads in its attitudes to war. The new way of war developed by the West over the last twenty-five years – to escape the dead-end of nuclear strategy and the degeneracy of the old way of warfighting in Vietnam – has failed. We have a choice: we can continue with war as a means, progressively abandoning the pretence that we are using armed force in new ways and becoming ever more mired in brutal struggles that we cannot win. Or we can follow the logic of our commitments to global institutions, democracy and human rights, and renew our determination to avoid war. We cannot have it both ways.

1

The New Western Way of War from Vietnam to Iraq

The new Western way of war that I examine in this book is the outcome of a long history of Western war. In contrast to some who see a technologically driven new way of warfighting at the beginning of the twenty-first century, I present the evolution of the new Western way in a broader social, political and military context. I argue that it evolved in response to the degeneracy of the twentieth-century Western way of war – with its tendency to target civilians rather than the armed enemy – and the specific crisis of the US war in Vietnam in the 1960s and 1970s. In this chapter I trace the latest United States wars in Afghanistan and Iraq through a history of 'new' wars, not exclusively American, from the Falklands to the Gulf and Kosovo campaigns. It is out of this historical experience, not some narrowly technological revolution, that the new Western way (which I summarize in chapter 4) has been forged.

The crisis of modern Western warfare

The new Western way is a development from modern Western war, the specific way of fighting industrialized total warfare that democracies – chiefly the USA and Britain – developed in the twentieth century. Although modern warfare classically centered on continental conflict between mass armies,[1] after 1914–18 many had dreamed of a 'cleaner' war in the air, which offered the possibility of avoiding the messy conflict that had produced the terrible slaughter of the trenches.[2] In Britain and the United States, especially, a model of 'liberal militarism' developed that increasingly relied on airpower, and more generally on high technology rather than mass armies.[3] In the mid-twentieth century, however, massive land engagements, with huge losses of life, could not be avoided. And airpower produced its own slaughter – of civilians as well as soldiers. The decisive episodes of aerial bombing by the Allied powers were extraordinarily destructive. Casualties from the notorious British bombing of German cities arose partly from the difficulties of precise targeting, given available technologies and the threat from anti-aircraft fire. But they also derived – and here was the reason for the controversy – from the deliberate adoption of indiscriminate 'area bombing' in order to break civilian morale. Likewise the first US use of the atomic bomb in 1945 targeted the civilian population in order to force the Japanese government to surrender. Despite some critical voices, Western publics largely accepted these atrocities, which seemed to follow from the all-out total war practised on all sides.

This was 'degenerate' war because, according to all the classic Western ideas and rules, war was supposed to be a contest between armed forces.[4] But it still worked as war since it remained possible to present it as a rational means to defeat the aggression of the Axis powers. However, when, from the 1940s to the 1980s, preparations for nuclear war generalized this idea of annihilating whole urban populations to the point of 'mutually assured destruction', it became increasingly difficult to claim that it remained rational. As Michael Howard pointed out, 'all traditional constraints on "absolute war" have been removed and its complete realization has for the first time become a practical possibility.'[5] Yet in reaching this limit, war also negated itself. If there were no longer internal constraints, and war became absolute destruction, it also became self-defeating, invalid as a means of policy. The Western way of war developed in the era of total war therefore faced a fundamental crisis, so that much of modern strategy could be seen as an attempt to avoid redundancy and to find uses for war in limited warfare, short of total nuclear war.[6]

In the first three decades after 1945, the more limited wars that were being fought were mostly rearguard actions by the old empires against national liberation movements in Asia and Africa. The British (Malaya, Kenya), French (Vietnam, Algeria) and Portuguese (Angola, Mozambique) fought often destructive campaigns against equally determined and ruthless enemies. In Vietnam the USA took on the mantle of colonial war, seeing in it the struggle to contain communism that had been bitterly fought in Korea in the early 1950s. Much 'counter-insurgency' warfare was necessarily on the ground, but wherever possible Western forces used their air supremacy to bomb extensively, inevitably killing the civilians among whom guerrillas hid. Political elites and publics mostly tolerated this harm: only a few episodes of murder and torture (such as the My Lai massacre) became *causes célèbres*. But when wars began to fail, and *Western* casualties seemed disproportionate to their results, publics revolted, as happened in France over the Algerian War and crucially in the USA over Vietnam. The futility of the American casualties (58,000 soldiers dead and many more wounded) and the crime of the far greater numbers of Vietnamese killed combined to make a whole pattern of warfare seem increasingly illegitimate. The use of napalm – followed by the brutal, extensive bombing of Cambodia – came to represent the inhumanity of airpower.

Vietnam was a watershed in the history of Western warfare, a moment when publics stood back from the kind of war that they had tolerated, and elites realized that war could not go on in the same way. At this point, the Western model of 'limited' war became as problematic as the model of 'absolute' war that had reached its crisis in the nuclear arms race. Underlying trends in world politics and Western society partially accounted for this crisis. By the 1960s colonial wars were ending, so that few citizens envisaged their states taking independent military action.[7] In Germany and Japan especially, generations had grown up in pacific cultures – initially enforced by the victorious Allies, but then internalized as national lessons about the dangers of aggressive militarism. To some extent, these were common European lessons that were learned by younger generations across the Continent. Moreover, changes in technology were changing the nature of war. Partly because of nuclear weapons, Western militaries no longer needed so many soldiers. The 'decline of mass armies' was a powerful trend,[8] masked by the anachronistic continuation of conscription in Western Europe.[9] Corresponding to this trend, young people were no longer socialized into the military: mass consumer societies became 'post-military' in the sense that most people's lives were not directly affected by military institutions and wars.[10] So the automatic social support for the military that had built up in the period of total wars began to fade away. People might find it easy to support military preparations that didn't seem to affect them – indeed, most of the time even the nuclear arms race attracted little attention. But when wars or weapons impinged on people's lives, as they did over Vietnam and at points of tension in the Cold War, opposition could be strong.

The Falklands-Malvinas War (1982)

It was after Vietnam that it became clear that Western warfare had to change from its classic modern form. For governments and militaries, it posed the challenge of how to continue using war without the costs that had so tarnished the reputation of that war. More broadly, it posed a problem of how to relegitimate war with publics. However, after the debacle of Vietnam, the USA had little interest in warfighting. By the early 1980s, it was preoccupied with the 'Second Cold War', the renewed arms race with the USSR, and few envisaged Western states being directly involved in wars. Moreover the arms race alerted publics once more to the danger of nuclear war, and led to a powerful new peace movement.

However, in many parts of the world local wars did not go away, and it was only a matter of time before Western states became involved again. The decline of 'national liberation' wars against European empires overlapped with a new pattern of wars in the Third World. Two main types of conflicts had developed, both with roots in post-colonial political structures: interstate wars between independent non-Western states (between Israel and the Arab states, India and Pakistan, China and Vietnam, Iran and Iraq); and civil wars between post-colonial states and armed opposition movements that claimed to be fighting for suppressed nationalities. None of these wars were simply results of the Cold War, but the inter-bloc conflict coloured them: the USA supplied money and arms to movements such as the Afghan mujaheddin, Angolan UNITA and Nicaraguan Contras. Both superpowers broadly backed Saddam Hussein's Iraq against the revolutionary Islamic regime in Iran: the politics of war were already more complex than the Cold War.

In this wider pattern, the 1982 war between the United Kingdom and Argentina seemed anomalous. However, when the government of Margaret Thatcher responded to the Argentine invasion of the British colony (in the Falkland or Malvinas Islands of the South Atlantic) by sending a large naval task force to reconquer them, it opened a new phase of Western warfare. The Falklands-Malvinas War[11] was the first serious war fought by a major Western state after the US withdrawal from Vietnam in 1975. Although the Falklands appeared to be an anachronistic colony, the tiny population of the islands (then 2,000) were almost entirely of British descent and supported British jurisdiction. The resort to war, first by the Argentine military junta in invading, and then by the United Kingdom in counter-invading, isolated islands – with modest strategic significance – whose future had been under negotiation between the two states, appeared just as anachronistic. This outcome was explained principally by the domestic political situations of the governments. The Argentine dictatorship used the invasion to rescue its threatened political base; Thatcher sought to rescue her government from the consequences of the intelligence and political failures that had allowed the invasion to occur.[12]

The peculiarities of the armed conflict arose mainly from its location. The battlespace consisted of the isolated waters of the South Atlantic, uninhabited and sparsely inhabited islands, and the skies above. British troops were based aboard the naval force until they landed on the islands; Argentinian air and naval forces, based on the mainland, attacked them, before the British surrounded and overcame the Argentinian garrison in the 'capital' (the settlement of Stanley) and hence reclaimed the colony for Britain. British forces did not attack Argentina itself, and the war was fought with conventional military forces, mostly based on the refined, complex and expensive weapons-platforms characterized by Kaldor as 'baroque'.[13] These updated Second World War systems – in Britain's case, as advanced as any available at the time – proved strikingly vulnerable to relatively inexpensive Exocet missiles, which sank the battleship HMS *Sheffield* and threatened other vessels. However, superior weaponry, training and intelligence (eventually reinforced by the USA) enabled the UK to prevail.

This was almost a textbook conflict between two sets of armed forces. As table 1.1 shows, 252 British and 655 Argentinian military personnel were killed, but only three Falkland Islanders and no Argentinian civilians.[14] There was criticism of the loss of life: many believed that, given the character of the islands and the nature of the dispute, no lives should have been sacrificed. Attention focused on the military decisions that exposed British soldiers to aerial attack and the British sinking of the Argentine cruiser *General Belgrano*, with over 300 lives lost. The ship was outside the UK's 200-mile 'total exclusion zone' at the time of the attack, and allegedly sailing away from rather than towards the British task force. The matter remained controversial in Britain for more than a decade, and Argentine sailors' families took the UK (unsuccessfully) to the European Court of Human Rights in 2000 in a bid to force their government to mount its own legal case in the International Court of Justice. Despite these criticisms, however, the war achieved high levels of popular support. The British campaign showed that a major Western state could successfully fight a war without the large numbers of casualties that the USA had suffered in Vietnam, and without losing public support.

British political and military elites had absorbed the understanding of the 'Vietnam syndrome' developed by their US counterparts, including their belief that television coverage had undermined the war though showing soldiers' 'body bags' to viewers. Although academic studies were to question this belief – media became critical of the Vietnam War only *after* it had started to go wrong and had become politically divisive in the USA[15] – policy-makers had learned the appropriate 'lessons'. The inaccessibility of the Falklands-Malvinas meant that media access was very difficult: the British government was able to make it dependent on the task force and restrict places to British journalists. Although international journalists could report from Buenos Aires, none could gain independent access to the war zone. Even more strikingly, the British government used control over satellite transmission to delay sending back pictures of the war. Through these measures the government achieved a level of domestic

Table 1.1 Estimated death tolls during and related to the 'major combat' phases of the new Western wars

	US and other Western military killed	Local allies' military deaths	Enemy military deaths	Civilians killed by enemy in precipitating events	Civilians killed by West	Indirectly caused civilian deaths as result of Western action
Falklands War 1982	252	n/a	655	3 (= total for war)	0	0
Gulf War 1991	327	Hundreds? (Kuwaiti resistance)	20,000–56,000	Hundreds or low thousands? (Iraqi invasion of Kuwait)	3,500	60,000–111,000 (health effects of infrastructure damage)
Kosovo War 1999	0	Hundreds? (KLA)	1,000	12,000 (Albanians)	500	Few?
Afghanistan 2001–2	1	Hundreds? (Northern Alliance/UF)	Thousands/tens of thousands?	3,000 (NY/DC)	1,000–10,000	3,200 (to end Jan 2002)
Iraq War 2003	172	Few? (Kurdish militias)	9,200	No such events ('pre-emptive')	3,750–9,900	Thousands?

Notes:
1 Figures refer to the 'major combat' phases only and do not include deaths after the conclusion of these phases.
2 'Civilians killed by enemy in precipitating events' refers to deaths during the acts of aggression that initiated the immediate conflict. It does not include the longer-term death tolls of earlier campaigns (e.g., Saddam Hussein's genocides, Serbian campaigns in Croatia and Bosnia, the Afghan civil war and Taliban repression) or subsequent war (e.g., Iraqi civil wars after the Gulf War, the elimination of the Marsh Arabs, etc.).
3 'Indirectly caused civilian deaths as result of Western action' refers to estimates of civilian deaths in the immediate aftermath of the war (e.g., civilian deaths as a result of the US destruction of infrastructure in Iraq and as a close consequence of the bombing of Afghanistan). It does not include longer-term deaths in which the war may have been influential (e.g., as a result of later sanctions against Iraq, or possible long-term consequences of the Afghan War).

Sources: Figures for Falklands War from <www.iwm.org.uk/server/show/ConWebDoc.1264> [25 August 2004]; Gulf War from B. Daponte, 'A Case Study in Estimating Casualties from War and its Aftermath: The 1991 Persian Gulf War', and C. Conetta, *The Wages of War*; Kosovo from International Independent Commission on Kosovo, *The Kosovo Report*; Afghanistan from C. Conetta, *Operation Enduring Freedom*, and A. Benini and L. Moulton, 'The Distribution of Civilian Victims'; Iraq War from <http://icasualties.org/oif> [25 August 2004], Conetta, *Wages of War*, and <www.iraqbodycount.net> [26 January 2004].

media control – and, by extension, global media influence – unimaginable in Vietnam.

Although in many ways this advantage reflected the war's unique location together with the early 1980s communications environment, there were crucial lessons for future Western wars. No later campaign could achieve the same degree of media control. But the idea of media *management* as a key to success was now established in the minds of Western political and military establishments. The British had not banned the media from the battlefield or practised extensive censorship. They had encouraged the presence of a spectrum of domestic television, newspaper and radio journalists. Twenty years before the term 'embedded journalists' was invented, they had bedded journalists very securely into the task force and made them dependent on the military.[16] Through this intervention in the conditions of news production, the British secured relatively favourable coverage that in turn helped lead to high levels of public opinion support. The government achieved a virtuous circle, influencing media coverage to produce positive reporting, which reinforced public support for the war, which in turn reinforced the tendency of journalists to report within a framework that legitimated the war. There was, a study of television news concluded, a parallel cycle at work among news producers: 'We have here a situation in which television selectively informs people's attitudes, then selectively reports on what those attitudes are, and finally . . . uses this version of public opinion to justify its own approach to reporting.'[17]

A new model of Western warfighting and media management had been established in a war in which civilian casualties were not an issue. Military casualties *were* an issue, but on the British side these were contained to a number that public opinion tolerated. The war was short (barely two months), decisive and successful. While particular incidents attracted controversy and deaths and injuries were viewed not only as sad and regrettable but also sometimes as unnecessary, these issues did not detract from the overall support for the war. As Lawrence Freedman was later to comment:

> It is widely assumed that modern democracies cannot tolerate great loss of life in support of goals other than direct defence of the country. This is held to be one of the major lessons of the Vietnam

war but it is founded on myth. . . . It was not pictures of 'body bags', of which there was precious little footage, that made television's role important, but the continual questioning by journalists of optimistic forecasts from the local military command.[18]

In the Falklands, there was little questioning, and the rapid conclusion of the war meant that questions did not seriously undermine its legitimacy. In the 1983 British general election, Margaret Thatcher gained a sweeping victory that was attributed largely to her success in the war.

The Falklands War was successful for the British government partly *because* the overall death toll was under a thousand – the 'entry' level that the well-known Correlates of War Project had set for an armed conflict to be counted as 'a war' in its study of wars up till 1980.[19] But the Falklands was a different kind of war, and showed that the criterion of a thousand battle deaths was outdated. Indeed another major Western campaign of subsequent years, in Kosovo, would see similarly low military and overall casualty levels. And although the others – the Gulf War, Afghanistan, and Iraq in 2003 – *would* count as wars on the Correlates criterion, this was because enemy and civilian deaths were much higher. It was the historically small death tolls among soldiers and sailors, in the context of initial legitimacy, speed and successful media management, which was the real key to why the Falklands 'worked' for Thatcher.

After the Cold War: the Gulf War (1991)

The Falklands had shown that Western states – while continuing to avoid 'hot' wars with major powers – could still fight wars against second- or third-rank non-Western states.[20] The importance of this lesson would become much clearer after the end of the Cold War. The Cold War wound down rapidly after the appointment of Mikhail Gorbachev as Soviet leader in 1985: a new superpower détente was developing by 1986, and the Soviet reform process soon stimulated democratic movements in Central Europe, leading in 1989 to the dramatic 'velvet' revolutions that overthrew the communist states in the region. These upheavals led to a far more radical transformation of world politics than Western leaders envisaged, and many of the effects seemed pacific. The democratic movements that overthrew communism in Europe also inspired the failed pro-democracy movement in China in 1989. They were matched by movements that overthrew pro-Western authoritarian regimes – in the Philippines and Latin America in the 1980s, and in South Africa, South Korea and Indonesia in the 1990s. In many other states, more gradual democratizations took place. Like Gorbachev, the USA mostly had little reason to oppose transition. Indeed from the late 1980s onwards it moved into active 'democracy promotion'.

However, the changes were not all benign. The dissolution of the USSR was marked by vicious wars between newly independent Armenia and Azerbaijan, and within Georgia, Moldova, Tadzhikistan and other successor states, including the Russian Federation itself (where the Chechen War has continued into the twenty-first century). The Yugoslav Federation also broke up in 1991, beginning a series of genocidal wars that lasted the decade. Freed from Cold War patronage and constraints, Ethiopia was divided after an independence war by Eritrean nationalists; Somalia fell apart, the prototype of the 'failed state' that became a recognized type, especially in Africa. Series of interlinked wars in central and western Africa saw state power often usurped by warlords and militia as well as abused by governments at the expense of civilian populations.

As the Cold War ended, the West was most exercised by the Soviet crisis; to a lesser extent by Yugoslavia; and much less by developments in Africa. However, all of these were eclipsed in June 1990, when the Iraqi dictator Saddam Hussein invaded the neighbouring oil-producing state of Kuwait. The central importance of Middle East oil to the Western and global economy meant that this was a very serious crisis. Although Saddam's regime had received tacit support against Iran, and despite its 1988 campaign against the Kurds, this new adventure was different. The threat of an unpredictable power controlling most of the Middle East's oilfields – if the Kuwaiti conquest held, Saudi Arabia could be next – made Iraq's illegal annexation intolerable. The humiliation of President George Bush's administration, which failed to foresee or pre-empt the Iraqi action, needed to be reversed, like

Thatcher's failure to prevent the Falklands invasion, by a decisive response. The clear-cut nature of Iraq's international violation meant that the USA could pose as the upholder of international law and mobilize UN support for action. The post-Cold War context enabled the war politically and militarily. Earlier it would have been inconceivably risky for the USA to launch a war against Iraq, a Soviet client state, and the USA's principal military assets were permanently tied up in the European theatre. Détente meant that it was possible to secure unprecedented Soviet support for military action, and to move large quantities of weapons systems and men from Europe and other arenas to the Middle East.

At last the USA could fight a war and show that, as Bush put it, it had 'kicked the Vietnam syndrome'. The Gulf War[21] was a full-blown Western war in that Britain, France and other European states participated, while Japan and Germany funded the conflict. It demonstrated the new synergy between the USA and the wider West on the one hand and the UN and an emergent 'global order' on the other. The US-led 'coalition' (the preferred term for the *ad hoc* alliance, also used in most subsequent conflicts) saw active participation by Saudi Arabia and other Arab states as well as passive support from the USSR and most states worldwide.

The Gulf War was, and remains, the biggest war that Western states have fought since Vietnam. It involved over half a million coalition and over a million Iraqi troops – almost twice the numbers in the 2003 war. It lasted six weeks, compared to a little over three weeks in the 'major combat' phase of 2003. Although all figures for Iraqi deaths in both wars are uncertain, it is clear that the 1991 war involved more casualties overall, as table 1.1 suggests. At least twice as many Iraqi soldiers were killed. Similar numbers of civilians were probably killed directly in both wars, but there were also huge numbers of civilian deaths due to the bombing of infrastructure (and also on account of Saddam's repression of insurrection, not included in the table) that were not repeated in 2003. Numbers of US and coalition soldiers killed were also greater (but only if we omit, as table 1.1 does, the post-war violence).

For the first five weeks, the Gulf War was almost exclusively an air campaign, with incessant bombing of Iraqi positions in Kuwait

and southern Iraq, as well as of Baghdad and Iraq's economic infrastructure. This weakened the Iraqi army, and minimized coalition
casualties when the ground war was launched. The Bush administration also limited its liabilities by agreeing a ceasefire with the
regime just when insurrections broke out in southern Iraq. Having
allowed Saddam's forces to continue using helicopter gunships,
the USA let its troops stand aside while they were used to crush
the rebels, sometimes even within earshot. The USA thus avoided
involving its troops in a messy civil war, or exposing them to the
kind of attacks seen during the 2003 occupation.[22]

The campaign utilized more precise methods of bombing and
saw the first large-scale uses of cruise missiles and 'smart' weapons.
Although there was much hyperbole, bombing *was* more dis-
criminating than in earlier campaigns. The US military remains
proud of its success:

> The combination of stealth technology, PGMs [precision-guided
> missiles], and satellite-aided navigation allowed precision attack as
> never before. Despite dropping 88,000 tons of bombs in the 43-
> day air campaign, only 3,000 civilians died directly as a result of
> the attacks, the lowest number of deaths from a major bombing
> campaign in the history of warfare. A key factor in explaining this
> low number was that US pilots abided by strict rules of engage-
> ment that required them to return with their bombs if unable to
> positively identify their military targets. As the commander of the
> operation, General Norman Schwarzkopf, said, 'We have been very,
> very careful in the direction of our attack to avoid damage of any
> kind to civilian installations. It's going to happen; it's absolutely
> going to happen; there's no question about it, but we're doing
> everything we can to avoid it.'[23]

Thus although civilian casualties did become an issue it was generally contained. Only two incidents threatened the generally
positive media coverage: the bombing of a shelter in Baghdad on
13 February 1991, killing several hundred civilians; and the
bombing of retreating Iraqi troops and their families on the
highway to Basra, on the last day of the US campaign. These massacres required serious 'spinning' by US spokesmen, but with the
support of pro-war media the uncomfortable visual evidence of
slaughter was explained away and its impact blunted.[24]

On all sides, the war was fought in the media. Saddam's strategy – after an initial public relations disaster showing him patting the heads of Western child hostages – was to repeat Vietnam, by causing enough American 'body bags' to force the USA to withdraw. The USA, on the other hand, had learned from the Falklands. It corralled most journalists at a US base in Saudi Arabia, where they were fed briefings; it restricted their presence on the battlefield to rotated outings with troops as part of a 'news pool' system; and it released film showing technological successes, not dead bodies. Only a few 'independents' ventured outside these controlled environments. The consensus of studies is that Western 'media management' was largely successful: coverage was mostly pro-war, public opinion remained overwhelmingly positive after fighting began, and the war was seen as a success for the participating governments.[25]

However, during the Kurdish refugee crisis which followed Saddam's crushing of the insurrections, the US and UK governments experienced serious 'blowback'. Although the history of modern war showed that defeated governments often disintegrate, and Iraq had always been ethnically, religiously and politically divided, Western governments had not planned for this eventuality. The British prime minister, John Major, even complained, 'I don't recall asking the Kurds to mount this particular insurrection.'[26] Nevertheless, the refusal of Turkey to countenance an influx of hundreds of thousands of refugees, combined with an effective campaign to aid the Kurds by some television and print journalists, forced Western governments to change their policy. The USA, the UK and France sent their troops back into northern Iraq to create a 'safe haven' and laid the foundations for an automous Kurdish enclave. The northern Iraq 'no-fly zone', in which US and UK planes prevented Iraqi intrusion, protected the enclave (a similar southern zone failed to make a difference since there was no comparable reality on the ground). Twelve years later, the two main Kurdish parties remained in control and were the USA's principal local allies in 2003.

The Gulf War thus tested the Falklands model under more difficult conditions. The striking differences were that this war involved extensive bombardment of large troop concentrations, and so caused far more enemy deaths; and it was fought against the mainland of a populated country and damaged the infrastructure on which civilians depended. It precipitated, in the short term, directly and indirectly, large loss of life among Iraqis (totalling over 100,000 on conservative estimates) while only hundreds of Western troops died. And yet this war was still popular in Western countries: President Bush counted it a success and was surprised to be ousted in 1992 (but he forgot that 'it's the economy, stupid'). Major was re-elected, against all odds: videos of him with the troops, wearing a flak jacket, seem to have helped his campaign.[27]

The 'success' was the result of a combination of factors, including favourable international and political conditions; limited goals; air supremacy and technological and strategic advantages; the minimizing of coalition and direct civilian casualties; and media management. Its specific, short-term 'success', however, has to be put in the context of the failed insurrections and the disastrous repression and suffering that they brought to the Iraqi people; the high death toll and suffering later in 1991 due to the destruction of water, sewage and electricity systems; the consequences of the failure to resolve the political and international impasse over the Saddam regime, which included debilitating sanctions and the impoverishment of many Iraqis over the following decade, as well as constant bombing to enforce the no-fly zones; and, ultimately, the 2003 war itself. Looked at in this light, there is no doubt that the word 'success' needs its inverted commas.

'Humanitarian intervention' and the Kosovo War (1999)

Throughout the 1990s, the Gulf War stood, like the Falklands War before it, as an apparently isolated example of major war involving Western states. It appeared that interstate war was not the main military problem facing the West. Instead, the problem of *managing wars* in the non-Western world appeared more important than that of waging wars. Although, as we have seen, both interstate and civil wars had been endemic in the previous period, they gained new Western attention in the aftermath of the Cold War. The reasons for this were twofold. Many wars fed by the Cold War had changed form, rather than simply disappearing in the

new climate – the basic conditions for these wars arose from contradictions in local power structures, rather than from the Cold
War itself. And the outbreak of wars in the regions destabilized
by the collapse of the Soviet system, especially Yugoslavia and the
USSR itself, created new war zones on the very margins of pros-
perous Western Europe.

In the early 1990s, therefore, there were actually *more* wars
and they were *perceived* differently from similar wars in earlier
decades, because there was no Cold War to consume most international attention. At the same time, the shift in Western policies
towards democracy-promotion created a more favourable climate
for human rights. Indeed the West had used 'human rights' issues
as part of its Helsinki-process negotiations with the USSR in the
1980s, so that there was already a presumption for taking them
seriously in the European context. This was consolidated globally
in new thinking within the United Nations in the early post-Cold
War years. In the short term, the US victory over Iraq and Bush
Senior's proclamation of the 'New World Order' created a synergy
between American power and global legitimacy. The seriousness
of the impasse in Iraq itself, and of the failure to make substantial institutional reforms in the global order, were not so evident
until later.

The human disasters on the ground in local wars were more
obvious. The Yugoslav wars, especially, shocked Western and UN
consciences, and led to more attention to human rights abuses,
extended (if not always very strongly) to other conflicts. Western
and UN leaders deplored these abuses but did not see them as
causes for military action. The initial failure of European Community mediation in the first serious Yugoslav war (in Croatia in
1991) led only to the deployment of a few UN peacekeepers. A
media exposé of concentration camps in Bosnia in 1992 led,
however, to an increased UN military presence. But the United
Nations Protection Force (Unprofor), with soldiers from France,
the UK and the Netherlands as well as non-Western states, existed
mainly to protect UN civilian operations (for example food
convoys to besieged communities) rather than to protect civilians
directly.[28]

In this case, 'humanitarian intervention' meant adding an armed
element to humanitarian aid. More generally, however, interven-

tion *was* held to involve actually protecting threatened civilians, and a doctrine of 'humanitarian intervention' evolved during the early 1990s. Although there were ample precedents from the 1970s interventions of India in Bangladesh, Vietnam in Cambodia and Tanzania in Uganda, all of which had halted major episodes of killing of civilians, 1990s thinking emerged from the new episodes in which the UN and Western states were involved.[29] The intervention in Iraqi Kurdistan was the key precedent; and at the end of 1992 President Bush, in the final days of his presidency, authorized a new US intervention in Somalia in order to save famine victims there.

This intervention, soon handed over to the UN, quickly turned into a disaster as local militias killed first Pakistani and then US troops. President Bill Clinton quickly withdrew US forces, and after this there was a period in which the idea of intervention was discredited. When forces within the Rwandan government and army launched their genocide against Tutsis and oppositionists in April 1994, the UN actually pulled out its small contingent, mainly Belgian soldiers, after some were massacred by the *génocidaires*, abandoning to their fate Rwandan civilians who had sought UN protection. Only after hundreds of thousands had been killed did UN officials in New York finally recognize that genocide was occurring, and even then the USA and other states stalled military intervention to halt it.[30] Subsequent apologies for their inaction by Clinton and UN Secretary-General Kofi Annan did little to compensate for the failure. Indeed, similar disasters were to occur in Bosnia, where in 1995 Dutch UN peacekeepers at Srebrenica handed over 7,000 men under their protection to Serbian forces who slaughtered them,[31] and in East Timor, where in 1999 UN staff abandoned civilians to murdering pro-Indonesian militia.

Thus in many situations of violence against civilians, effective intervention was lacking. Neither the UN nor the West consistently applied the 'emergent norm' of 'humanitarian intervention'; this term did not accurately describe the range of UN and Western military actions. For example, in Bosnia, after further Serbian massacres in 1993, the UN Security Council declared six remaining threatened towns 'safe areas'. However, the implied protection was never properly supported by military power, opening the way to the 1995 massacre. The UN's failures led Clinton to impose the Dayton settlement of 1996, following which a NATO force was installed to control what became a UN protectorate. Although this halted the killing, it also froze most of the gains of the genocidists, allowing Serbian nationalists to keep their own republic as an 'entity' within Bosnia-Herzegovina.

These changing uses of military power were not, therefore, expressions of a singular 'humanitarianism'. Troops variously 'protected' aid convoys, UN civilian personnel, and sometimes local civilians. They were used to enforce settlements that prioritized political compromise over the rights of victims. Only in the final stages of the Bosnian war did the USA use really coercive military power, in bombing Serbian positions around the capital, Sarajevo. At least as important as these US actions were the gains of the Croatian and Bosnian armies, trained and partially supplied by the USA, at the expense of Serbian forces. And the bombing remained 'demonstrative', indicating the new US commitment to achieve a conclusion to the war rather than fully confronting Serbian forces.

The Dayton settlement in Bosnia left unresolved the original conflict in Kosovo, the province ruled by Milosevic's Serbia to the exclusion of its 90 per cent Albanian majority population. Albanians had pursued a policy of peaceful civil resistance throughout the 1990s.[32] However, their failure to win concessions from Serbia or meaningful support from the West led some to form the Kosovo Liberation Army (KLA), which after Dayton began a campaign of violence against Serbian state institutions. By 1998 there was serious warfare between the KLA and Serbian forces, which responded with a brutal counter-insurgency campaign, burning villages suspected of hiding KLA fighters. Over the next year 2,000 were killed and tens of thousands made homeless. The USA attempted to mediate with Milosevic, and when this failed tried to force the parties to a settlement at Rambouillet, near Paris, in early 1999. Milosevic resisted this settlement and risked the threatened NATO bombardment.

The NATO air campaign that began on 24 March 1999 was intended, like earlier attacks on Serbian positions in Bosnia, to show the alliance's determination. 'Demonstrative' air strikes against Yugoslav military and official positions, in Serbia and Kosovo, did not constitute an all-out attempt to *force* Serbia to halt its attacks on Albanians, let alone to relinquish its control of Kosovo. The numbers of raids and quantities of ammunition were small compared to those involved in the opening days of the Gulf War, and showed no intention to impose victory. In any case, airpower alone could not directly affect the situation on the ground in Kosovo. The Gulf had shown that ground forces were still needed, but over Kosovo Clinton had ruled them out and foolishly made this public knowledge. The theory was that Milosevic would 'understand' that he had now to give in and even use NATO's campaign to 'sell' this outcome to public opinion. Instead he understood, more accurately, that NATO was not fully serious and that it could not stop his forces doing what he wanted in Kosovo. So Milosevic called NATO's bluff, with a campaign of terror in which probably 10,000 Albanians were killed and the majority of the 2 million population were driven from their homes – forced to flee from Kosovo (fleeced by Serbian troops at the border) or into its more mountainous regions.[33]

It was therefore Serbia's response that forced NATO to fight an increasingly serious war. Ostensibly, NATO had intervened to protect Albanian civilians and force Serbia to a political settlement that recognized their rights; latent goals included facing down Milosevic, the prime mover of the post-Yugoslav wars, and demonstrating NATO's own capacity. But 'demonstrative' air strikes had backfired disastrously, as extensive media coverage of the plight of refugees (in camps in Macedonia and Albania) constantly reminded the alliance's leaders and publics. If NATO was to avoid total humiliation, it had to escalate its military action in response. However, neither Clinton nor most European leaders would deploy ground troops. The escalation could only be a wider and deeper use of airpower, so the numbers of raids and bombs were increased and targets widened to include more questionable economic sites, risking civilian lives to a greater extent.

In the three months of the campaign, as table 1.1 shows, around 500 Serbian and Albanian civilians were killed (not many fewer than the small numbers of enemy military). By historical standards, and even compared to those in the Gulf War, the numbers were small. However, in a war that was partly 'humanitarian' in purpose – and had become more so, since now the restoration of the refugees was an overriding priority – the civilian bloodshed was shocking. Accidental massacres, for example of passengers on a train and of refugees in a convoy, embarrassed NATO even more than similar incidents in 1991. The legitimacy of this 'collateral damage' was greatly undermined by the fact that the alliance was not prepared to risk exposing the bombers themselves to Serbian anti-aircraft fire. NATO risked civilian lives through high-altitude targeting errors in order to keep its aircrews safe. The strategy's complete success – not a single member of the NATO military forces lost his life through enemy action – only underlined its moral and political questionability.

The one-sided, exclusively aerial nature of NATO's campaign has led some to question whether the conflict was a war. Indeed NATO Secretary-General Javier Solana confusingly proclaimed: 'Let me be clear: NATO is not waging war against Yugoslavia.'[34] Likewise, NATO commander General Wesley K. Clark said: 'This was not, strictly speaking, a war.'[35] And, like the Falklands, the NATO–Serbia conflict alone probably fails the 1,000 battle deaths criterion. However, this ignores the fact that a war had actually been going on since early 1998, between Serbia-Yugoslavia and the KLA; NATO *intervened in* this war in March 1999 and brought it to a conclusion in June that year.[36] (The episode as a whole clearly saw more than 1,000 battle deaths.) NATO's use of force worked, if not directly by destroying Yugoslav armour, then indirectly by inducing economic, political and diplomatic pressure on the Serbian regime.

Moreover, Kosovo was the ultimate manifestation of the trend to use violence while reducing the risk to the West's own forces to the minimum. Awkward civilian casualties were sidelined by the willingness of surviving Albanians to accept that NATO's killings were genuinely accidental, a price worth paying for overthrowing Serbian domination and restoring them to their homes. Even in Serbia, where the bombing was far less accepted, much of the blame was placed at Milosevic's door. Thus when in 2000 a popular uprising overthrew the dictator, anger was focused on officials who had knowingly placed television workers in the line of an expected NATO attack. In Western Europe and North America, although there was much criticism, the lack of Western casualties meant that ultimately the war was not deeply challenged.

Although Kosovo had not been the same kind of all-out military struggle as the 1991 Gulf War, it was another example of the new Western way of using war in international politics. It showed that 'humanitarian intervention' and war were not totally different types of use of military power. There was actually a spectrum of practices, from the most limited type of 'humanitarian' or peacekeeping action, through more contested peace-enforcement, to a serious war like that in the Gulf. Although the oxymoron 'humanitarian war' should be rejected, it reflects Kosovo's location on the spectrum, more 'war' than many 'humanitarian' actions, but a less complete use of force than the Gulf campaign. And of course the Kosovo War was succeeded, as had been the more limited bombing campaign in Bosnia, by a NATO occupation. Here there was a different Western division of labour from the war itself: while the USA provided most of the bombers, European and other UN states provided most of the longer-term forces on the ground in the liberated province.

The Global War on Terror: from Afghanistan (2001) to Iraq (2003)

The Kosovo War almost closed the decade of wars in former Yugoslavia: finally the West imposed a significant defeat[37] on its prime mover, Slobodan Milosevic. A year later he was overthrown and shortly afterwards was sent for trial before the International Tribunal at The Hague. Also in 2000 war broke out between Albanian nationalists (inspired by the KLA) and the Macedonian government, but this, uniquely, was brought under control by Western diplomatic intervention. Regional elites now looked more towards integration with the European Union than to war. Of course the end, for the time being at least, of the Yugoslav wars did not end local wars worldwide. The remaining regions of war, although involving appalling atrocities and huge numbers of deaths – millions may have died from violence and disease in the Congo[38] in the late 1990s – engaged less central Western interests. Nevertheless there were still cases in which Western states became involved. In the early 2000s, the United Kingdom intervened to end the civil war in Sierra Leone and France undertook similar operations in both Ivory Coast and the Congo, but none of these constituted a large-scale 'war' on the part of the Western states.

The strand of 1990s war that came to pose the most direct challenge to Western interests was given only modest attention during that decade. In 1993, Islamist militants attempted to bomb the World Trade Center in New York; in 1998, militants of al-Qaeda, led by Osama bin Laden, bombed the US embassies in Nairobi and Dar-es-Salaam, killing over 200 people and injuring 4,000, mostly Kenyans and Tanzanians; in 2000, they attacked the USS *Cole* off Yemen, killing seventeen US servicemen. The 1998 bombings provoked President Clinton to order missile attacks on a pharmaceuticals factory in Sudan, believed (erroneously) to be an al-Qaeda weapons factory, as well as a base in Afghanistan. However, despite this record, the threat of Islamist 'terrorism' did not become a central concern of US military policy until the terrible massacres of nearly 3,000 people in the World Trade Center and the Pentagon on 11 September 2001.[39]

The US response to 9/11 opened up a new phase of Western warfare. The attacks did indeed constitute 'acts of war', as President George W. Bush described them. However, they were also crimes in both US and international law, and the al-Qaeda network that carried them out was embedded across the Western world as well as in Muslim states. A campaign against it could never rely solely on military means; it would have to apprehend many conspirators through domestic and international law-enforcement. Nonetheless, President Bush lost no time in pronouncing his 'war' on terrorism. There was little doubt that he meant war literally as well as figuratively: given the enormity of the 'act of war' against the USA, only war seemed a proportional response.

Thus the *idea* of war against terrorism came before it was clear even who the enemy was, or how a war might be prosecuted. Official commentary emphasized the novelty of the Global War on Terror and critics noted the anachronism of a 'war' against a phenomenon. However, the Global War was not so much a war as a *political and ideological framework* that would legitimate any specific war upon which US political leaders wished to embark. As such, the model was the Cold War, in which the central military enemy, the Soviet Union, had also represented an 'ism', communism. Anti-communism could legitimate action against anyone tarred with the communist brush, as liberals, social democrats and others were from time to time. The difference, in the Global War on Terror, was that the central military enemy, al-Qaeda, was much weaker and more nebulous than the USSR, and the military struggle was not calibrated in an overt arms race. This looseness of the framework meant that it offered even more flexibility than the Cold War. Al-Qaeda was almost the perfect enemy: capable of wreaking real destruction that rightly strikes fear into all those who inhabit capital cities or fly between them, but not (as was the USSR) of totally destroying the USA. Its unpredictability increased its significance as a mobilizer of fear. It could be neither wholly defeated nor negotiated with, so it would remain a permanent spectre.

The pull of the Global War on Terror was more uncertain, however, than that of the Cold War. At one level it was stunningly universal: al-Qaeda and similar groups have carried out bomb attacks from Saudi Arabia to Indonesia, and threatened most Western countries and their citizens. All states that were fighting secessionist wars against enemies that could be labelled 'terrorist' saw an immediate advantage in the framework. From India to Israel and the Philippines to Russia, they tried to cash in a political advantage with the USA. However, while similar threats created an incentive for political and policing cooperation, they did not compel *military* alliance in the way that the threat of Soviet invasion used to. Indeed the US preference, as we have seen, is for loose 'coalitions' rather than formal alliance – NATO has been used only in the former Yugoslavia. But the trouble with coalitions is that governments can opt out as well as in. Although the first phase of the Global War on Terror, in Afghanistan, easily pulled in most of the USA's Western partners, the second, in Iraq, saw major abstentions. The reason for the difference was simple. In the aftermath of 9/11 there was strong solidarity with the USA. As the presumption of al-Qaeda's involvement was followed by confirmation, the US counter-attack seemed legitimate to most states and public opinion worldwide. Moreover, 'war' was quickly operationalized as a campaign against al-Qaeda's main bases in Afghanistan and its protectors and allies in the Taliban regime that ruled the country. This had a general plausibility as 'self-defence'

in international law, and gained support from some who had criticized earlier Western wars.

The attack on Iraq was different. No provocative action by
Saddam Hussein precipitated the US attempt to overthrow him.
His regime continued to suppress its people, but its major crimes
were in the past, and this was not the argument made for the war.
Although his government was in breach of UN resolutions, it represented no immediate threat to other states. The USA cut short
new UN inspections of Iraq's weapons programmes when they
seemed to be effective. Connections made in US propaganda
between Saddam and 'terrorism' lacked evidence: to most they
were simply implausible. The framework of the Global War was
shown to be just *too* flexible in the Iraqi case. The justification of
the war was not traditional international law but a radical new
doctrine of 'pre-emptive war'. It was not surprising that the
French, German and Russian governments, which had backed the
USA over Afghanistan, recoiled at the attack on Iraq.

It makes sense, therefore, to evaluate Afghanistan and Iraq as
two distinct wars. The Afghan War was improvised by the US military within four weeks of 9/11. Starting on 6 October 2001, US
and British planes bombed Taliban positions in Kabul, Kandahar
and other places, as well as al-Qaeda bases. Precision-guided
munitions, targeted by special forces on the ground, enabled the
Northern Alliance–United Front, the Afghan opposition already
fighting on the ground, to break the stalemate in their long war
against the Taliban.[40] Intensive bombing, with the benefit of complete air mastery, quickly weakened Taliban forces so that the
opposition were able to take Kabul by 13 November. As in the
Gulf and (after a slow start) in Kosovo, 'bombing worked'.[41] A
weaker enemy than any the West had faced in its other wars[42]
abandoned its hold on major centres, and a pro-US government
was quickly established. However, despite the tonnage of high
explosives expended on them, the more determined al-Qaeda
forces were not routed. They melted into mountainous tribal
regions and continued a guerrilla war. Significant fighting persisted
long after the symbolic 'victory' in Kabul – indeed it carries on at
the time of writing over two years later. And the problems of the
pro-US government were not confined to al-Qaeda. Because the

USA had relied on the opposition to defeat the Taliban, its victory strengthened opposition warlords in some parts of the country, so that the new central administration had only modest purchase on power even in regions where the Taliban were eliminated.

The quick first phase in Afghanistan – the 'war' as far as the media was concerned – was thus conventional ground warfare by the Afghan opposition, reinforced by US bombing and thus almost casualty free for the USA in the Kosovo way (see table 1.1). Up to late January 2002, the only US official killed by enemy action was a CIA operative killed in a prisoners' rebellion in Mazar-e-Sharif. Conservative estimates of civilian casualties in the same period gave at least 1,000 dead from US bombing and over 3,000 from indirect causes;[43] a study based on community surveys on the ground suggested even higher figures for deaths from this phase of war, even up to 10,000, including victims of unexploded ordnance and mines.[44] Since bombs were not directed *at* civilians, except when enemy fighters were believed to be in civilian areas, or by mistake, it seems likely that – as in the Gulf and Kosovo wars – as many, if not more, enemy combatants must also have been killed. In the aftermath of 9/11, there was no public concern about the bombing of Taliban fighters, however lightly armed, and no reliable estimates of their death toll exist. Civilian casualties were mostly accepted as the 'accidental' and 'unfortunate' price of defeating terrorism.

Even when more coalition troops were killed and injured in the pursuit of al-Qaeda into more remote border areas, overall numbers were still smaller than in the Gulf War, and did not bring the war's 'success' into question. However, avoiding risk to US troops may have compromised military effectiveness:

> Military commentators suggest that reluctance to use troops on the ground is a consequence of the risk aversion of American leaders. In the case of Afghanistan, in particular, it is argued that had more American troops been committed in the battle for Tora Bora (December 2001), or later to Operation Anaconda (an operation in March 2002 in the Shah e Kot valley where al-Qaeda operatives were hiding), Osama bin Laden would not have got away, even though many more Americans might have died.[45]

The USA had overrelied on local allies who were not as committed or effective, just as it relied on its Western allies, other states and the UN to provide the bulk of peacekeeping and civilian forces.

These difficulties could be seen partly as specific consequences of pursuing 'terrorists' in mountainous terrain, or of the nature of Afghan society and its history of armed conflicts.[46] However, they also reflected, more than in Kosovo, the difficulties of relying on local allies to supply the ground war. Ground war remained an important element in warfare, and it could be subcontracted to allies, even with special forces support, only where allies were both available and militarily capable. The implications for Iraq, where the administration's aim was 'regime change', were considerable. Before the Iraq War, it was reported that 'Military planners in the Bush administration are arguing that they have learned the lessons of Afghanistan and that [US] ground troops will have to be used and casualties accepted.'[47] But it was nevertheless clear that the USA was relying on the established model of war that contained these casualties within a politically acceptable level.

Conclusion

This survey of the Western wars of the last two decades has shown many peculiarities of particular conflicts, but also many emerging common themes. Through the Falklands, the Gulf, Kosovo and Afghanistan, Western states had re-established a viable way of fighting wars after the crisis of Vietnam. But on what, exactly, was this way of war based? How should we best characterize and explain it? How did it relate to earlier Western ways of war and what, indeed, constitutes a distinctive 'way of war'? And, most importantly, can this way of war continue to work? How well has it survived its most serious test to date, the ambitious project of regime change in Iraq? These are the questions that we shall pursue in the remainder of this book.

2

Theories of the New Western Way of War

The story of the new Western wars in the last chapter showed both common features and development from one war to the next, but the wars differed significantly from each other. Wars are never routine social events, always large-scale historical dramas. Historians see them as unique episodes, and war studies tend towards the descriptive because it seems difficult to generalize. Even if we recognize a larger pattern, each war makes us see it in a new light. So although there has been a growing tendency to see something new in Western warfare for the last twenty-five years, some identify the Falklands and Gulf wars as part of an 'old' way superseded in Kosovo, Afghanistan and Iraq; others see Iraq as marking a new phase compared to Kosovo. Therefore it is important to probe further the idea of a new Western way of war.

The most obvious meaning of this idea is the *general pattern in the actual practice of warfighting* by Western states. However, the relationship between warfighting and war-preparation is a fundamental issue here. Is the 'Western way of war' just the method of warfighting, or does it refer to *the larger way of organizing military and political power* that lies behind it? What is the relationship between the way Western states fight the limited wars that we have described, tightly limited in time and space, and the military machines that they maintain – which we know to be huge and, including nuclear weapons, potentially far more destructive than anything we have actually seen in recent years? What are the relationships between ways of warfighting, military organization, and social and political structure? To ask these questions makes us realize that understanding a 'new Western way of war' is not as straightforward as it seems. Just pulling out 'dimensions' from the descriptive account in chapter 1 would beg the question of what constitutes a way of war, which deserves to be examined in its own right. We cannot simply derive a new theory of the 'way of war' from the history. Rather we need to look first to the existing theories.

A Western way of war

It is obvious that each army has its own way of fighting, which changes over time. There are national military traditions, and these develop. However, it has also been plausibly argued that there is a common 'Western way of war'. The historian Victor Davis Hanson traced its origins from the ancient Greek idea of 'the daylight collision of armed soldiers', through Clausewitz's idea of 'hammer blows' or the absolute destruction of the enemy's armed forces in the field: 'It is this Western desire for a single, magnificent collision of infantry, for brutal killing with edged weapons on a battlefield between free men, that has baffled and terrified our adversaries from the non-Western word for more than 2,500 years.'[1] Hanson saw modern Americans as the principal heirs to this tradition, protagonists of combat rather than manoeuvre, their armies most dedicated – especially in the Second World War – to direct assault and frontal attack.

However, Hanson emphasized crucial differences between ancient Greeks and modern Americans. The Greeks fought brutal battles in order to *confine* killing in time and space, to substitute battle for more destructive war: 'its moral imperative is to end the fighting quickly and efficiently, not simply to exhibit brave resolve.'[2]

> To the Greeks who long ago formulated these ideas about battle, anything less than a 'fair' fight – that is, a daylight clash of two massed phalanxes, was no fight at all. . . . [The] deliberate dependence on face-to-face killing at close range explains another universal object of disdain in Greek literature: those who fight from afar, the lightly equipped skirmisher or peltast, the javelin thrower, the slinger, and above all, the archer. These were all men who could kill 'good' infantry with a frightening randomness and little risk to themselves.[3]

The problem, Hanson argued, was that 'our general ideas about the conduct of battle even under the frightening conditions of contemporary warfare have not changed much . . . from those practiced by our Greek ancestors.'[4] Our ideas of battle have remained much the same, although 'the mechanics of pitched infantry battle' from which they derived are 'now nearly obsolete'. In continuing this tradition, 'The stark simplicity of Greek combat, bereft of heroics and romanticism, has not been appreciated by us, their Western heirs.'[5]

The results of this disparity could be seen, Hanson pointed out, in the slaughters of the Somme and Omaha Beach. Meanwhile, the method had become 'embarrassingly ineffective' in guerrilla wars such as Vietnam where the enemy sought 'not to engage in *but rather to avoid infantry battle*'.[6] And we could hardly approach a nuclear exchange in the spirit of 'grim resolution to have the fighting done quickly and effectively with a minimum of casualties':[7]

> There is a terrible danger in the nuclear age to all of us who see this very legacy of the Greek manner of warfare surviving and living on well past the demise of actual infantry battle and the moral climate of its birth, a climate with which it was once so uniquely designed and integrated.[8]

Thus Hanson concluded this discussion with the challenge: 'Have we not seen then, in our lifetime, the end of the Western way of war?'[9]

The sense of the end of a period in warfare, encouraged by the end of the Cold War itself as well as post-Vietnam disillusionment, was common to much commentary in the 1980s. Hanson's critique of the continuation of Greek ideas into modern strategic thinking highlighted, however, issues that were to become central to the 'new' Western wars. In these wars, as we have seen, it is not only the enemy who 'avoid infantry battle': this has been, until Iraq at least, an objective of all recent United States campaigns. 'Those who fight from afar, . . . kill[ing] "good" infantry with a frightening randomness and little risk to themselves', now included US pilots as well as guerrillas and terrorists. Americans were no longer among the Greeks of modern war, but among the Persians, who 'in Herodotus' view . . . suffered from that most dangerous tendency in war: a wish to kill but not to die in the process.'[10] So if there was a new Western way of war, it had hardly resolved the moral dilemmas of the old.[11]

Moreover, Hanson's 'Western way of war' was too simple as a historical concept. If Greek warfare was 'uniquely designed and integrated' into Greek society, the modern Western way of war – with both its nuclear weapons and its moral deficiencies – must surely be understood in the context of modern Western society. And if there was a *new* Western way of war, it too must be understood in its changing social context. How to grapple with this relationship, of warfighting and its sources in social relations, was the methodological challenge for contemporary scholars.

The revolution in military affairs

Strategically, however, the novelty of contemporary Western warfare has been seen mostly in very different terms, concerning the impact of technology on warfare. The Gulf War's 'smart' weapons provided the major stimulus to this debate. Most of the literature focused on the *potential* of new technologies to transform war further than that war had shown. The information-technology-led transformation was variously named 'hyperwar' and 'cyberwar',[12] but the label that stuck was the 'revolution in military affairs' (known in military policy circles by its acronym, RMA). Analysts of this 'revolution' focused not only on the new precision of weaponry itself, but also on the comprehensive transformation of communications, command, control and intelligence systems. And the more sophisticated versions of the thesis recognized that, as Thomas Keaney and Eliot Cohen argued, 'Technology alone does not a revolution make; how military organisations adapt and shape new technology, military systems and operational concepts matters much more.'[13] Or, as Andrew Latham put it, 'the advent of "intelligent" weapons, while important, is not the most significant military consequence of the information revolution. Even more transformative has been the development of a military "information infrastructure" that allows masses of real-time information to be collected, collated and distributed almost instantaneously.'[14]

The significance of the new technology was that it enabled the United States to gain a qualitative advantage over its main rivals, the more so since the Soviet Union had collapsed and China, often seen as the emerging long-term rival, was unable to compete with the USA on its own terms. In any case, the most likely short-term enemies were 'rogue' states and armed movements that could not hope to match US military power. The conclusion drawn from such inequalities was that the future lay with 'asymmetric war'.[15]

These new concepts sent their proponents scurrying back into history, analysing earlier historical revolutions equally centred on new technologies and their complex consequences. As Keaney and Cohen summarized:

> revolutionary change in the conduct of war requires the advent or maturation of new technologies (e.g. the internal combustion engine, armor, etc.), their integration into new military systems (e.g. the tank or long-range bomber), the adoption of appropriate operational concepts (e.g. the armored breakthrough and its adaptation), and finally the requisite organizational adaptation (e.g. the *Panzer* division).[16]

However, for some this pattern, of repeated technological changes associated with wide-ranging organizational and tactical changes, was less impressive. An influential conservative school of 'classical realist' strategic thought saw these as adaptations rather than 'revolutions' in military affairs. For Colin Gray, the conduct of an 'RMA' had to be examined as a form of strategic behaviour, which means that, of necessity, it must 'work' as strategy works. Gray was sceptical towards the RMA debates since for him 'modern' strategy was essentially a given doctrinal framework, established by Clausewitz 170 years ago and still fundamentally valid.[17] Clausewitz's concepts were essentially 'timeless' truths about modern warfare – unlikely to be outdated in the way that Hanson proposed, and not subject to any drastic revision in consequence of the latest computer technologies. From this point of view, there was unlikely to be a *fundamentally* new way of war, Western or otherwise, for the simple reason that the dilemmas of war remain the same, regardless of changes in social, political and technological circumstances.[18] In the same vein, Vincent J. Goulding pointed out that 'asymmetric warfare' was hardly a novelty of the present period: 'ironically, it's a concept as old as warfare itself.'[19]

The new American way

Thus, although the RMA idea developed in the strategic community that straddles US military and academia, many theorists have not been so impressed with its claims. Even those who believed there was significant novelty in contemporary Western warfare defined it in terms much broader than technology. Thus Eliot A. Cohen, reflecting on Kosovo, proposed that the 'old American way of war' had given way to a 'new American way'. For him, the old way was encapsulated in the call for 'fighting spirit' and 'killing mood', even blood 'lust', made by a Second World War commander.[20] Its four defining qualities were similar to those that Hanson identified in the historic 'Western way': extreme aggressiveness; the quest for decisive battle; discomfort with ambiguous objectives, constricted resources and political constraints; and a clear-cut understanding of civil–military relations in which the tasks of soldiers and politicians are discrete and well recognized.[21] For Cohen, the Gulf War was not so much a departure as the swansong of this old American way. Even Kosovo 'did not represent a conscious abandonment of this tradition. . . . But the war did illustrate the extent to which modern conditions had rendered that tradition inadequate and, indeed, obsolete.'[22]

The new American way of war, then, was born of changing conditions. It led the USA to fight wars over issues that were not 'for concrete, vital interests' but for secondary or even tertiary interests, and to defend its reputation. It led US leaders to abandon the strict distinction between political *goals* and military *means*; instead every aspect of the war was political. And it steered the USA into war 'leading coalitions into battle, . . . over the space of a century it has made itself a remarkably adroit leader of multinational military enterprises.'[23] The new American way was thus (even if Cohen did not use the term) the new Western way: 'The purely unilateral way of war died in the United States a long time ago.'[24]

The new American way was defined, therefore, as much in political as in technological terms. However, it did have a distinct operational style: air power had become 'the weapon of choice for American statecraft'. This was the result of two crucial technological developments. The first was the 'the routinization of precision': 'by any historical standard the technological advance in weapons accuracy has been immense: after centuries of warfare in which the vast majority of ordnance expended hit nothing except unoccupied land or sea, today most weapons actually hit their intended targets.' The second was 'the ability to employ weapons against an adversary without suffering losses, except very rarely and indeed almost by accident. . . . In many cases, American airpower can operate with near impunity.'[25]

However, these advantages were not without their drawbacks: 'as precision becomes technically possible, it quickly becomes politically imperative: accidents as an inevitable byproduct of war become less acceptable. Public opinion abroad and at home, diplomatic reactions by foreign governments (allied, neutral and hostile alike) are all less forgiving.'[26] Indeed, Cohen noted that

> Reliance on airpower (albeit a radically different kind of airpower than the bludgeon of World War II strategic bombing) represents some elements of continuity with the old American Way of War. The same cannot be said of the changed American attitude towards ground combat. Here too, a combination of training and technology have produced what is, from one point of view, tremendous increases in military effectiveness. . . . Assuming, that is, that Americans are willing to use them. . . . When, as occurred earlier in the Yugoslavia intervention, US commanders tell their troops that the first mission is force protection, this represents a fundamental change in American attitudes to ground warfare. . . . It appears in fact that the American military has become more sensitive to casualties than civilians.[27]

'Casualty sensitivity', therefore, was 'first and foremost' among 'the vulnerabilities inherent in [the new American] way of war', combined with 'deference to allied opinion' and 'an unwillingness even to contemplate serious land operations'. Such a way of war, Cohen admitted, may be 'strangely successful': Kosovo's 'bloodless victory [*sic*] . . . marked a new milestone in an era that has evoked a new way of war.'

This hypothesis of change was qualified by the assertion that 'no way of war is a fixed thing. Under the right set of circumstances leaders and their society may accept very different styles of conflict. But barring some cataclysmic event – a twenty-first century Pearl Harbor – it seems likely that the [new] American way of war will prevail for some time to come.'[28] The qualification now seems prescient, but it raises a crucial question. If a new 'way of war' (Western and not just American, since allies were integral to it) was crystallizing at the end of the twentieth century, before 9/11, did the Global War on Terror mean that all bets were off? Cohen himself has suggested that they were, becoming notorious for his description of the Global War on Terror as World War IV.[29] I shall argue, however, that reports of the death of the emerging 'new way of war' were premature: it lived on in ever-newer guises. Before we decided if it had passed on, we needed to work out more fully what it was.

Spectator-sport, virtual and virtuous war

Strategists do not – and should not – have a monopoly on thinking about war. Changes in wars' relationships to society are quite as important as changes in how wars are actually fought in battlespaces.[30] Strategists tend to see society as non-essential background, but wars are always profoundly important social events and social relations are not just context. They enter in many ways into the organization, fighting and consequences of war. Not surprisingly, sociological debates anticipated today's strategic revisions by at least a decade, reflecting as early as the 1970s and 1980s on the fundamental changes that were transforming warfare. Military sociologists analysed the 'decline of mass armies': as Western militaries became more capital-intensive, with sophisticated technologies incorporated into weapons and platforms, they required fewer but more skilled personnel.[31] Soldiers in 'all-volunteer' forces were specialist workers, and with them came the shift to an 'occupational' military with increasingly 'civilian' conditions of service.[32] And these changes had profound implications for how wars could be fought. Skilled professionals, in whom militaries made considerable training investments, could not be treated as cannon-fodder.

This was one source of the 'force protection' that strategic commentators now emphasize. The other, however, lay in the ways in which wars were represented and managed within the media and political spheres of Western societies. In the aftermath of the Falklands War, British sociologists reflected on these conditions. Robin Luckham pointed out that the structural trend from labour- to capital-intensive militaries had wide-ranging cultural ramifications. The glorification of military institutions and values was replaced by the cult of the weapon-system: traditional militarism was replaced by 'armament culture'.[33] Michael Mann argued that mass-participation militarism had been replaced in the West by the privatized 'deterrence-science' militarism of the elites and the 'spectator-sport' militarism of the masses.[34] Summing up this literature, I suggested that a 'post-military society' was emerging in the West, in the sense that traditional forms of military mobilization and participation had been transcended. This trend would only deepen in the post-Cold War era.[35]

Clearly, this did not mean an end to war, but war would be very different in a post-military society. The Falklands-Malvinas War appeared an exceptional episode, but it had shown a new way of fighting war. Mann had exaggerated when he wrote that, as a media event, this kind of war was 'not qualitatively different from the Olympic Games'.[36] Likewise Jean Baudrillard overstated his case that 'the Gulf War did not take place': it was just a media event.[37] A study of public opinion in the 1991 Gulf War suggested that viewers still grasped the difference, fearing the violence of the far-away bombing campaign.[38] However, the idea that war could be fought *with* blanket media coverage but *without* many casualties, which were mostly not actually shown to viewers, became mainstream with the Gulf War. Studies of media management became a standard accompaniment of the new Western wars,[39] although few analysed the cases in which management became problematic, such as Kurdistan in 1991.[40]

Mann's idea of the 'spectator-sport' aspect of new Western wars has been widely reproduced: thus, for Emmanuel Todd the American way is 'theatrical micro-militarism'[41] and for Mary

Kaldor it is 'spectacle war'.[42] Michael Ignatieff's study of Kosovo introduced the idea of 'virtual war', virtual not only in its complete replacement of ground war with bombardment and its lack of Western casualties, but also in its popular mobilization, its public consent, its alliance structure[43] and even its victory. He too went so far as to assert that, 'When war becomes a spectator sport, the media becomes *the* decisive theatre of operations.'[44]

> Because virtual wars are fought on camera and are directed primarily at the opponent's will to fight, Western military commanders know that success is now contingent on public acceptance. In fact, there is no such thing as a purely military success: a success which takes out a target but leaves behind moral or political debris is a strike which has failed. The military's response to sharpened moral and political exposure has been to call in the lawyers.[45]

Ultimately, Ignatieff concluded, in such virtual war, it was the West's values that risked being seen as inauthentic. As Paul W. Kahn put it, 'Riskless warfare in the pursuit of human rights' was a moral contradiction.[46]

Yet the success of the new Western way of war, James Der Derian argued, was how it appeared to overcome this problem:

> On its own, virtualization does not embody a revolution in diplomatic or military, let alone human, affairs. However, deployed with the new ethical and economic imperatives for global democratic reform and neo-liberal markets, it could well be. In spite of and perhaps because of efforts to spread a democratic peace through globalization and humanitarian intervention, war is ascending to an even 'higher' plane, from the virtual to the *virtuous*. . . . At the heart of virtuous war is the technical capability and ethical imperative to threaten and, if necessary, actualize violence from a distance – *with no or minimum casualties*.[47]

The core contradiction was 'that virtuous war is anything *but* less destructive, deadly or bloody for those on the receiving end of the big technological stick.' It was just that violent conflict underwent 'virtual cleansing'.[48] Der Derian tried 'to comprehend how the sanitization of violence that began with the Gulf War has come to overpower the mortification of the body that marks communal wars in Nagorno-Karabakh, Somalia, Bosnia, Rwanda, and elsewhere. Virtuous war is many things: a felicitous oxymoron, a form of deterrence, a growing paradox, an ominous sign of things to come. Yet in the final analysis that it seeks to evade, virtuous war is still about killing others.'[49] Der Derian's book 'mapped' the interconnected military–media networks of virtuous war, through which 'the way we fight and report wars converges onto a single screen of electronic representation.'[50] He argued not just that war had become virtual/virtuous, but that we needed a *virtual theory*, 'constructing an interaction' between the objective and subjective, exploring 'how reality is seen, framed, read and generated in the conceptualization and actualization of the event.'[51] We were in a permanent interwar condition; the interwar was 'eternally returning'.[52] And no theory 'could possibly convey or bridge the regret, despair, horror of an undeserved death.'[53]

Thus the presumption of most arguments about a 'new Western way of war' was that this was different from what went on elsewhere. Western military power has been discussed in isolation, although Western campaigns were mostly responses to attacks by non-Western states or armed movements, either on the West itself or on civilian populations. Der Derian reminded us that, however terminologically and visually 'cleansed', Western wars were still wars, killing civilians as well as armed enemies. Yet the differences still seemed to matter. The distinctiveness of new Western wars was that they generally no longer targeted civilians as a way of attacking the enemy state. The 'precision' of new Western weapons was accompanied by more serious attempts to distinguish military and civilian targets than ever occurred in earlier periods. Thus the significance of continuing civilian deaths was that they occurred *despite* and even *because of* these *new* methods and ideologies of Western wars. The challenge for theory was to grasp this contradictory new reality and *not* to reduce it to some pre-existing model.

Ways of war, modes of warfare

Nearly twenty years ago, I wrote that 'the defect of most social theory of war and militarism is that it has sought to reduce war to rational, material interests: it has not considered war as practice, i.e. what people actually do in war. Hence again, "the active side has been developed abstractly" – in this case by military theory.'[54] It is evident from the above discussion that most critical social theorists now recognize wars as active projects of states and militaries, which cannot be explained away by interests, structures or ideologies. Likewise, strategists increasingly recognize the reality of the social, political and media contexts in which Western states fight their wars, even if their focus is on the fighting. To this extent, there has been a welcome convergence of strategic and social thought.

And yet capturing the new Western way of war has brought us up against the old dilemma in a new way. Strategists such as Cohen, emphasizing military doctrines, have been relatively uninterested in the social networks that facilitate new wars. For a critical social theory, this remains a sticking point – thus critics such as Der Derian have emphasized the sprawling 'military–industrial–media–entertainment network'. Strategists have tended to share the military's inability to see clearly the West's victims as part of the new way of war; sociologically minded critics have tended to conclude, like Der Derian, with the 'undeserved deaths' that remain. Thus there were both theoretical and moral, and maybe also political, differences between these approaches. They would not go away, and the argument of this book is clearly on the critical sociological side.

However, there remains a tension between examining *wars* as projects and *warfare* as a social institution, which refers to a real issue in understanding. In order to grasp this issue it is useful to refer, once again, to Clausewitz. For three main reasons, he remains the pivotal figure for social theory's engagement with strategy.[55] First, he presents war as a type of social action, which is compared with others such as commerce. Therefore his framework is in principle open to understanding the parallels between, and connections of, war and other types of action. Second, his writings contain a clear conceptual representation of the inner logic of war, linking elements such as political objectives, supply, deployment, environment and battle within an understanding of the whole. In principle, again, this means that the links in the strategic chain can be connected to other social institutions. Third, his writings contain a primitive sociology that begins to address these connections: for example, the famous comparison between battle and exchange as moments of 'realization' in war and commerce respectively; and the connections between social forces (government, commanders and people-in-arms) and the elements of his famous 'trinity' of war (rationality, chance and violence).

Thus although Clausewitz is the founder of modern strategy, as understood by conservative 'classical realists' such as Gray, his ideas are open to more critical uses.[56] The most fruitful development of Clausewitz's ideas was Mary Kaldor's.[57] She used his framework to define the 'mode of warfare' as analogous to the mode of production: a rational, goal-oriented arena of social action comparable, as such, to the system of production for profit. For her, warfare had its own *irreducible* character and ends: thus the 'mode of warfare' should be distinguished from the 'role of warfare' in the mode of production. And by contrast with orthodox Marxists, who often saw warfare as necessary for capitalism, Kaldor saw its distinct logic as a *problem* for capitalist accumulation. War was an 'a priori burden on and potential interruption to the process of capitalist accumulation. This tension between warfare and capitalism explodes periodically in war.'[58] The enormous demands of a permanent arms race distorted the economy and accentuated crisis. The absence of actual war made the mode of warfare ever more artificial, overblown and rigid, which increased the pressure for war simply to test weapons and military plans. And yet war as a means was obviously self-defeating: no sectors of capital could actually have a rational interest in nuclear war.[59]

In insisting on the centrality of warfare to modern society and its non-reducibility to production, Kaldor was in line with neo-Weberian social theorists such as Giddens, who saw 'warfare' as one of four core 'institutional clusters' of modern society,[60] and Mann, who defined military power as one of the four 'sources of social power'.[61] What all these theorists did was to pinpoint a broader, deeper concept of warfare as a type of power and a complex of relations, processes and institutions in modern society. Kaldor's concept was particularly interesting because Clausewitz gave her a framework for understanding the active side. Her specific understanding of the 'mode of warfare', ambitiously theorizing a tension that threatened nuclear war, may be outdated. However, the idea of a 'mode of warfare' survives as an alternative to the notion of a 'way of war' that has been used in the literature reviewed earlier in this chapter. Although 'mode' and 'way' have similar general meanings, we should employ these terms quite differently in the social science of war. Thus I use 'mode of warfare' to describe *the general complex of social relations, processes and institutions through which wars are prepared, military power organized and wars fought* in a given society and historical period. In contrast, I shall retain the term 'way of war' to refer to *a particular way of organizing war adopted by an actor or group of actors.*

Ways of war in total warfare

To make this distinction clearer, I shall briefly examine how these categories can be applied in understanding industrialized total warfare, the historic mode of warfare of modern industrial society. Industrialized total warfare combined 'total' social mobilization – extensive reorganization of national societies for war – with 'total' destruction – targeting of civilian populations as well as mass armies. These two elements of total war were crucially linked: social mobilization incorporated economy and society into the 'supply' side of war, which in turn created the demand to treat them as 'targets'. Technological dynamism supplied ever more destructive means, enabling this military 'logic' to be realized, while mass politics and thinking supplied the rationale for treating civilian populations as part of the 'enemy'. The connection of civilian targeting to the core logics and dynamics of the total war mode meant that in general it produced 'degenerate war'. [62]

It is clear even from this brief summary that, as a 'mode of warfare', industrialized total warfare could not be understood independently of its connections with other social 'modes', 'domains' or 'clusters'.[63] Twentieth-century industrialized total warfare depended on the nineteenth-century development of industrial capitalism, mass politics, mass media, etc. For many social scientists, this might confirm the 'normal' assumption of the primacy of socio-economic explanation. But the subsequent history of industrialized total warfare suggests a unique sense in which warfare came to *structure* economy, polity and culture, and (especially in the world wars) to *dominate* them and *override* economic, political and cultural logics. The 'normal' assumption is thus brought into question. However, since there is no universal law of military any more than of socio-economic determinism, we should regard the dominance of military power as a specific historical phenomenon of early twentieth-century society. We need to see whether and how this has changed in twenty-first-century conditions.

It is also clear that discussing a mode of warfare in this way is different from discussing particular wars. I have discussed total warfare as a *general complex* of social relations, processes and institutions through which wars were prepared, military power was organized and wars were fought in twentieth-century world society. Clearly this is different from how total war has been discussed in the historical literature, as the *actual practice* of war in 1914–18 and 1939–45.[64] Both uses are valid: to understand the larger 'mode', we clearly need a take on the actual practice of war – and vice versa. The point is, of course, that each war is a very distinct episode, or set of events. We saw in our discussion of the new Western wars in chapter 1 that each war had many individual characteristics. The wars of 1914–18 and 1939–45, although classified together as 'world wars', were actually very different from each other. Indeed as gigantic world events, involving dozens of states and hundreds of millions of people, they were actually 'composite' struggles, each involving many distinct wars and episodes. The Second World War, for example, involved not only the conflict of the Allied and Axis powers, but also many other wars. In China, for instance, the war between the Allies and the Japanese empire overlay the Chinese war against Japanese occupation and the communist Chinese war against the Kuomintang; and, similarly, complex regional and local struggles were taking place in many parts of Europe and Asia. Guerrillas and resistance fighters, armed civilians as well as formal combatants, fought alongside armies, navies and air forces.

Alongside the distinctiveness of specific wars must be set the question of the relationship between war and 'interwar' periods. In retrospect, we easily label 1918–39 the interwar years: this was not so obvious at the time, at least not before the mid-1930s, when people started to regard another great war as inevitable. And yet we can also easily see this interwar period, and later the Cold War, as part of the larger period of total warfare, the short twentieth century. We are right to do so, because the social, political, technological and military dynamics of total warfare continued to operate in these periods. However, they did not operate in the same way during interwar years as during the world wars themselves. The relationships between the 'mode of war' and economy, polity and culture were balanced quite differently in war and in interwar. The actual outbreak of war always sharply changed the dynamics, just as did the outbreak of 'peace'.

Moreover we can assert that there were distinctive *ways* of practising war in the era of total warfare, and these belonged to different *actors* or classes of actor. Of course, actors themselves have sometimes drawn sharper distinctions than were justified between their own and their enemies' modes. But even if some of these distinctions were self-serving (thus the victorious Allies' criminalization of Axis ways of fighting served to take attention away from their own atrocities), some distinctions have been widely accepted in the literature. The Japanese and German invasions of China and the Soviet Union respectively have been understood as uniquely aggressive forms of land warfare that the Allies did not match; likewise it is widely acknowledged that the Allies' bombing in the second half of the war, while a response to earlier bombing by the Axis powers, represented a new climax in aerial destruction. Both were generally 'degenerate' in the sense of targeting civilians as part of the 'enemy', but in different ways resulting from different aims. Thus where violence against civilian populations was informed by the aim of destroying certain groups in society 'as such', it constituted something more than degenerate war, which we call 'genocide'.[65] Likewise it is generally accepted that guerrilla war was a distinctive way of fighting, the main method of parties (such as the Chinese and Yugoslav communists) that were struggling for state power, even if it overlapped with more 'conventional' total war and was also practised or supported by major states.

I therefore propose that we could distinguish Western, totalitarian and guerrilla as the principal distinctive ways of warfighting in the era of industrialized total warfare, as shown in table 2.1,

Table 2.1 Ways of war in industrialized total warfare

Protagonists:	*Principal ways of war against:*			
	Western democratic states and civilian populations	Totalitarian states and civilian populations	Armed political movements and supporting civilian populations	Civilian social groups as such
Western democratic states		Strategic bombing > nuclear war	Counter-insurgency, oppression	
Totalitarian states	Destructive invasion + strategic bombing > nuclear war		Counter-insurgency, oppression > destruction	Oppression > destruction
Armed political movements	Guerrilla war			Oppression > destruction
General types of war:	*Degenerate war*	*Degenerate war*	*Degenerate war*	*Genocide*

while acknowledging that these distinctions are schematic. However, these were all variants of, or different ways of prosecuting, total war, sharing the defining characteristics identified above. All three were conditioned by each other, as the different actors developed their ways of war in bitter struggle in the two world wars and other conflicts. Thus we can combine the framework of the total 'mode' of warfare with recognition of the distinctiveness of different ways of warfighting. Table 2.1 is offered in this spirit, as an indication of how this approach might be developed, rather than as a final model. From this basis, we can approach the question of the contemporary Western way of war. It follows from the conception that I have developed that we need first to think about the contemporary mode of warfare in general, before we can come to definitive conclusions about the Western way. This is the aim of the following chapter.

3

The Global Surveillance Mode of Warfare

Existing literatures focus chiefly on the new Western or American way, as we saw in the last chapter, or on 'new wars' among non-Western states and armed movements. It seems difficult to conceptualize Western and non-Western warfare together in a single frame. However, there is an overriding case for doing so. All Western military campaigns, we have seen, are directed against non-Western states and armed movements. They generally respond to conflicts in non-Western regions if not to actual attacks on the West. And Western interventions have fundamental impacts on the course of non-Western wars. A sharp distinction between Western and non-Western wars or warfare is therefore impossible to sustain.

Beyond this, the most superficial examination shows that weapons, communications systems and other technologies of war are diffused through worldwide markets. Even the most irregular armed forces organize their political and financial bases through worldwide networks. There are global patterns of military organization in which both West and non-West are involved. There is, I shall argue, a global mode of warfare that embraces the organization, practice and thinking of war worldwide, and is articulated with the economy, polity and media of the emerging global society. This mode and its articulations are complex and segmented, but they have significant unitary qualities.

The world military order and military globalization

The basis for understanding the world organization of warfare as a whole is little developed. There are useful collections of

information, overviews of statistical trends and geographical patterns,[1] but few attempts to provide general explanations. The term
'world military order' has been used to describe these patterns and
to suggest the linkages between developments in the advanced
industrial regions and the Third World.[2] And one of the few conceptually developed overviews, by David Held and his colleagues,
suggests that there has been a process of 'military globalization',
embodying 'the growing extensity and intensity of military relations among the political units of the world system'.[3] With
modern 'time-space compression', centres of military power
worldwide have been brought into 'closer proximity and potential conflict, as the capability to project enormous destructive
power across vast differences has proliferated.'[4] The military order,
Held et al. suggest, is *global* for three reasons: the worldwide reach
of great power rivalry, the development of a global arms dynamic,
and the expansion of global governance of military affairs.[5]

Military globalization in these senses is not unique to the current period. Warfare has become increasingly globalized throughout the modern era, and indeed the experience of war has been
one of the factors leading people across the world to recognize
their common 'global' situation and history. Thus there are important continuities between contemporary war and earlier periods
of modern warfare. However, Held et al. do identify three distinctive 'new' trends in the military relations, towards

1   a growing gap between the military capabilities of the USA
    and other major military powers, combined, however, with
    decreasing military rivalries between major powers, and with
    more fragmented local and regional rivalries;[6]
2   an expansion in the number of states with weapons-manufac-
    turing capabilities and involved in arms export, combined with
    a transnationalization of Western defence industries;[7]
3   growing global and regional governance, with more interna-
    tional security regimes leading to the increased management
    of war.[8]

Contemporary globalizing trends involve, therefore, both commonalities – the spread of weapons-production and governance –
and segmentation – the disparities between the USA and other

powers, and between major powers and local armed actors. Moreover, on this account, changes in the military order are linked closely to political changes, among them the collapse of the USSR and the growth of regional and global institutions; and to economic changes, including the commercialization of arms production and the growth of transnational production.

This account of the world military order highlights how *embedded* military systems are in otherwise pacific world political and economic systems. However, the study of military systems, concentrated on weapons and manpower capabilities, military expenditures and organization, etc., does not indicate – in any simple or straightforward sense – the pattern of actual armed conflicts. In the global era, the study of ongoing wars produces very different results from that of military expenditure and organization. A map of worldwide power in which states are pictured according to the size of their military expenditure shows a bloated USA, while Africa appears tiny.[9] Yet a map of actual wars will show the North American continent unscathed (apart from 9/11) while Africa is covered with many long-lasting, ugly, murderous wars.

Thus the West is more dominant – as are large states generally – in military production than in warfighting. This is mainly because many of the huge military expenditures and sophisticated weapons systems prepare for wars that, in practice, are not fought. The greater part of all military organization and production is not actually used in war for long periods, if at all. Nuclear weapons systems have consumed billions of dollars and man-years of political, scientific and military time, but none have been used since 1945.[10] Nor is this only a matter of nuclear weapons. The costs of big wars *generally* inhibit major states from risking them. During the Cold War, although leaders on both sides engaged in preparations to use nuclear weapons, they simultaneously avoided concrete steps towards use. In today's world, with a larger number of nuclear-armed states, a similar reluctance is widespread. The USA maintains a capability theoretically sufficient to fight not just Iraq and North Korea but Russia and China simultaneously,[11] but in practice it is difficult to conceive of circumstances in which this might occur.

However, the decline of warfighting between major states is due to more than the costs of nuclear and other weapons. It reflects major changes in the structure of global power. Since 1945, 'Western' states have no longer fought wars of any kind against each other, even though they remain economic rivals. This is not primarily because, as advocates of the 'democratic peace' thesis contend, democracies are inherently more peaceable than authoritarian states.[12] Rather it is because the USA, the major European states and Japan knitted together a network of permanent multilateral institutions, political-economic as well as military alliances, through which their interdependence was consolidated. Other major (non-Western) states such as China, India and Pakistan have fought wars against each other in the past and continue to engage in serious border conflicts. However, the extension of global governance, US and UN monitoring, and the growing economic costs of war in conditions of global interdependence combine generally to deter war between major states. Like the superpowers in the Cold War, great and nuclear powers today prepare extensively for interstate wars that in practice they avoid.

Thus the dominant position of the West in military production and capacity does not fully specify how *wars* themselves continue to be reproduced. We might be tempted to unravel this paradox by suggesting that war is produced in the advanced West, but fought in Africa and other non-Western regions. But the evidence does not give simple support to this idea. We saw in chapter 1 that all the 'new' Western campaigns except the 2003 Iraq War were fought in response to aggressive acts by non-Western states either against the West or against other regional actors. A list of the major wars in the last fifteen years (table 3.1) confirms that Western states and the UN have been direct protagonists in only a small proportion of recent wars. In most cases, the West and the UN have been involved only in limited military 'interventions' in *ongoing* wars between local and regional powers; or they have not been concerned in a direct military role at all, but only in a political or diplomatic way.

Obviously the classification of particular cases could be argued about, but the general pattern is quite clear. Most wars are fought primarily among local and regional actors rather than between these and the West. The West is usually involved, to a greater or lesser degree, in the political conflicts surrounding these wars, but they are invariably rooted most directly in local and regional

Table 3.1 Maximum forms of Western–UN involvement in selected wars since 1990, by region

Post-Soviet	
Armenia–Azerbaijan	political and diplomatic
Georgia	political and diplomatic
Moldova	political and diplomatic
Tadzhikistan	political and diplomatic
Chechnya	political and diplomatic
Post-Yugoslav	
Slovenia	political and diplomatic
Croatia	military intervention
Bosnia-Herzegovina	military intervention
Kosovo	*major protagonist in war*
Macedonia	military intervention
Middle East	
Israel–Palestine	political and diplomatic
Iraq 1991	*major protagonist in war*
Iraq 2003	*major protagonist in war*
al-Qaeda–USA	*major protagonist in war*
Africa	
Angola	political and diplomatic
Sudan	political and diplomatic
Ethiopia–Eritrea	political and diplomatic
Somalia	military intervention
Rwanda	military intervention
Congo–Zaire	military intervention
Liberia	military intervention
Sierra Leone	military intervention
Ivory Coast	military intervention
Asia	
Afghanistan to 2001	political and diplomatic
Afghanistan 2001–	*major protagonist in war*
Kashmir	political and diplomatic
Cambodia	military intervention
East Timor	military intervention
Indonesia	political and diplomatic
Nepal	political and diplomatic
Philippines	military intervention
Latin America	
Colombia	military intervention

Note: 'military intervention' includes limited armed actions or troop deployments short of all-out war; 'political and diplomatic' indicates significant but wholly or largely non-military intervention.

power cleavages. In this sense, war is produced as well as fought in the local political structures of the non-Western world, although these are connected in many complex ways to the global structures that link West and non-West.

New wars and Western wars

Thus the processes that limit major interstate wars are less generally successful in restraining unofficial armed movements and states' responses to them. There is widespread warfare, as table 3.1 reminded us, even if most of it involves the West only in a secondary sense, and even if it utilizes only a small fraction of military expenditure. The costs of small arms – machine-guns, Kalashnikovs, hand-launched missiles – hardly figure in global military-expenditure accounting, but they do enormous harm in many wars. We need to encompass the variety and complexity of the warfare that is being waged or planned in the current era in any adequate understanding of the contemporary mode of warfare.

No wonder then that most theorists and students of war have shied away from any such inclusive task, tending to maintain the Cold War division between strategic studies (concerned with war-preparation between major states) and development studies (concerned with economic and political change, and until recently often ignoring the many wars in the Third World). The welcome 'merging of development and security'[13] in recent years has, however, started to produce systematic knowledge of ongoing wars, pointing towards a global integration of war studies. A useful starting point – especially significant given the author's role in originating the 'mode of warfare' concept – is Mary Kaldor's concept of 'new wars'.[14]

Against the grain of widespread assumptions that most 1990s wars were merely 'civil' wars produced by 'ethnic conflict' and that there was a simple 'privatization' of violence, Kaldor clearly demonstrated that 'ethnic' wars were political conflicts, involving state power as well as various 'private' forces, in which 'identity politics' was a means for elites to reproduce their power. Kaldor showed how this functioned in a new political economy of war, in which a range of new militaries – the decaying remnants of state armies, paramilitary groups (often financed by governments), self-defence units, mercenaries and international troops – engaged in violence against civilians, including the systematic murder of 'others' and forcible population expulsion known as 'cleansing'. Unlike the classic modern war-economy of the total-war nation-state – which was mobilizing and production-oriented – the new 'globalized' war economy was demobilizing and parasitic, a 'predatory social condition'. It damaged the economies of neighbouring regions as well as the zone of warfare itself, spreading refugees, identity-based politics and illegal trade. It created 'bad neighbourhoods' in world economy and society – regional clusters such as the Balkans, the Caucasus, the Horn of Africa, Central Africa, West Africa, Central Asia and of course the Middle East.

Kaldor argued that the global context was crucial to understanding this new political economy of war. Violence was reproduced through an 'extreme form of globalization' in which production collapsed and armed forces were sustained by émigré remittances, diaspora fund-raising, external governmental assistance and the diversion of international humanitarian aid.[15] Thus transnational networks were integral to new wars. In turn, protagonists in these wars obtained their weapons in globalized arms markets, rather than through domestic manufacture. Internationalized Western-global interventions (by NGOs and media as well as militaries) were another form of globalization. Mark Duffield argued that these Western interventions were modes of 'global governance' characterized by new 'liberal strategic complexes', involving state and non-state actors, chief among which he identifies NGOs, donor governments, multilateral agencies, military establishments, the corporate sector and academics.[16]

However, the same 'global' forces that Kaldor and Duffield identified in 'new wars' affected 'Western wars' too. These were *not* two different types of war: we have seen that 'new wars' often led to Western 'interventions' which sometimes became 'new Western wars' (as in Kosovo). Likewise Western 'wars' generally required 'interventions' (policing, humanitarian aid, reconstruction) in their aftermaths, and if these were unsuccessful they led to further messy phases of 'new war' (guerrilla war and counter-insurgency). Western and non-Western warfare took place within the same environments: the same zones of war, the social and political spaces in which armed force is used, and a global political–military environment.

Transition to the global mode of war

What we need therefore is a more comprehensive account of the contemporary mode of war, within which the relations of different actors, ways of war, phases of war, and military environments can be understood. One way of approaching this question is to ask *how* the old total mode of warfare was transformed. However, Kaldor offers us less on this, since she mistakenly defined 'old' warfare as Clausewitzian and argued that 'new' wars are 'post-Clausewitzian'.[17] She conflated military doctrines with modes of warfare and types of war, narrowing the new mode of warfare to one particular type of war and simultaneously underestimating the continuing significance of Clausewitz's ideas for the theory of warfare.[18] But if a mode of warfare is a general complex of social relations, processes and institutions through which wars are prepared, military power organized and wars fought in a type of society, then it cannot be defined by a particular *doctrine* of war.

The transition from industrialized total warfare is perhaps more obviously approached from the point of view of changes in the West. Andrew Latham emphasizes links between the technological dynamic and the emerging desiderata of 'precision' with 'the decline of the mass army and the shift to smaller, more flexible and increasingly professional armed forces', and also with a new 'economy of representation' – an 'imaginary' in which 'rogue states' replaced the old Soviet enemy.[19] The RMA, he argues, 'is less a "rational" reaction to changes in technology and the emergence of new "threats" than it is a cultural artefact of the end of the Cold War and the emergence of a new, discursively constructed threat to Western (and especially US) security.'[20] However, insofar as Latham considers the 'new' mode of war exclusively from the point of view of the new Western – indeed, largely American – 'way' of war, he also narrows the perspective, although in a different way from Kaldor.

Our starting point, therefore, must be a broader historical explanation of the transition from industrialized total warfare to the new mode. The central shift is the one that began in the West during the Cold War, but has now become increasingly worldwide: from *direct* to *indirect* mass mobilization. It is not only Western states that no longer need mass armies, mass production, mass politics and tight media control to fight wars. At the other extreme of global-era warfare, armed movements can also operate without the formal military organizations, the control of the countryside, the mass peasant support and the dedicated propaganda machines that characterized mid-twentieth-century guerrilla movements. Western states fight wars with (relatively) small professional armies, relying on more specialized, high-tech weapons industries, public-opinion control and media management. The new type of armed movement operates informally and underground, some-times without even attempting to achieve control of territory, reaching its constituency through the Internet, by distributing videotapes and penetrating mass-media coverage.

The core of the new mode of warfare is therefore a different general relationship between warfighting and the political, eco-nomic and cultural-ideological domains. I suggested in chapter 2 that industrialized total warfare came to structure economy, polity and culture, and sometimes to dominate them and override 'normal' economic, political and cultural logics. The 'total' nature of war meant that economy, polity and culture tended to be incor-porated into the mode of warfare.[21] Total warfare had the capac-ity to *dominate* society: it could override market relations, suppress democratic politics and capture media for substantial periods. Global warfare in contrast is generally *subordinate* to economy, polity and culture. It becomes locally dominant in war zones, and even globally dominant for brief periods, but it cannot override social relations as fully or widely as total war could. On the con-trary, global warfare must nestle in the interstices of polity, economy and culture. States and other armed actors must make war work in political, economic and cultural as well as strictly mil-itary terms. Wars must play much more by the rules of politics, markets and media: warmaking must *capitalize* on market rela-tions, *exploit* democratic political forms, and *manage* independent media. In the end, armed actors must reckon not so much with global governance – which suggests a purely governmental even if broadly based process – but with the comprehensive surveillance of their military ventures by global state institutions, law, markets, media and civil society. The best way of characterizing the new mode of war as a whole is therefore *global surveillance warfare*.

Table 3.2 shows some of the main dimensions of the 'old' and 'new' modes of warfare and the changing political, economic and cultural systems on which they depend. The table is designed to show how the 'new' features of global-era warfare are connected to 'new' global politics, economy and media. It aims to show, too, how the Cold War nuclear war-preparation was a transitional phase between industrialized total warfare and contemporary global warfare. During the Cold War there was a gradual transformation of the total warfare structure of the relationships between war, economy, polity and culture. Nuclear war-preparations still formed a dominant, 'overarching' structure, possessing a clear potential to override other social dynamics – indeed to wipe them out, 'exterminating' social life.[22] However, this extreme dominance became increasingly abstract compared to the comprehensive, concrete dominance of warfare over society in the period of the world wars. Nuclear war-preparations abandoned the mobilizing side of total war, and so the logic of nuclear war weakened the tendency of warfare to dominate. The war-induced statism of the twentieth century went into reverse, with the liberalization of Western and world economies in the second half of the Cold War. While these shifts were commonly linked to the rise of 'neo-liberal' ideology and the political 'New Right' in the Reagan–Thatcher era, their necessary precondition was the changing nature of warfare. For the full emergence of a new mode of warfare, however, it was necessary to break down the Cold War political structures that kept nuclear total warfare going.

The consolidation of a Western–global power conglomerate at the centre of the world system, harnessing the United Nations to its goals, meant that armed conflicts worldwide were increasingly subject to a multi-layered system of political surveillance: by the USA and other Western states, in the UN, and through the prism of international law. The other political consequence was

Table 3.2 The transition from industrialized total warfare to global warfare

	Industrialized total warfare (WWII)	Industrialized total warfare (Cold War)	Global surveillance warfare (post-Cold War)
Core interstate relations and conflicts	inter-imperial (multipolar)	inter-bloc (bipolar)	Western–global state congolomerate vs. 'rogue' states, 'terror' networks (unipolar)
Secondary interstate relations and conflicts	national movements vs. empires	national movements vs. old empires and new quasi-imperial states	national movements vs. quasi-imperial states
International law, global institutions	weak (League of Nations)	neutered (UN in Cold War)	developing (post-Cold War UN, international tribunals, ICC)
Most advanced weapons technology and platforms	conventional explosive bombs, aeroplanes	nuclear warheads, missile-delivery systems	computer-aided precision munitions; integrated command, control, communications
Most advanced armed forces	conscript	volunteer	professionalized volunteer
War ideology	democracy, communism vs. fascism	democracy vs. communism	democracy vs. terrorism
Politics of non-Western world	colonialism	authoritarianism, military rule, Stalinism	democratizing, semi-authoritarianism
World economy	imperial zones, autarchic regimes, limited free trade	partial Western world economy, limited free trade	globalizing, expanding free trade
National economies	statism, planning, welfare states	internationalization, marketization	globalizing national economies
Media technologies	radio, newspapers, cinema	television	multi-media, Internet
Media control	national control	internationalization of national media	global and regional media markets

democratization, increasingly a goal of Western and global institutions as well as of local reformers and oppressed groups.
Although partial, contradictory, contested and by no means
universal, democratization also opened up the potential of media
and civil society as parallel sources of surveillance in wars. These
political outcomes were reinforced by the economic outcomes
that they facilitated. The Western-dominated world economy
expanded to the entire globe, opening up the largely closed communist states, including China, to global market participation.
Within an emerging global economy, national states retained
important levers and collectively made the rules through global
institutions and law, but their success depended on competition.[23]
Together with expanding formal democracy, the spread of market
relations also made possible a rapid growth of mass media, as well
as of parties, non-governmental organizations, social movements
and other institutions of civil society. More open markets enabled
media and civil society to operate more than ever before in a
global context. Emerging global media and global civil society
were greatly reinforced by the development of multi-media global
communication, aided by the technological revolution associated
with mass computing. Indeed the Internet meant that individuals
and small groups worldwide, as well as institutions and organized
groups, could participate in surveillance. Surveillance is often
thought of as one-way, but in fact it is increasingly the gaze of
all over all, even if some gazes are more influential than others.
This increasingly global surveillance has huge implications for all
warfighting.[24]

The end of the Cold War particularly facilitated the emergence
of a new Western way of war, after the crisis of Vietnam. The
West now dominated world politics unequivocally without
having to worry about the Soviet Union. Linkage to the nuclear
danger was no longer ever-present in Western regional interventions. Thus wars became more practicable: the end of the Cold
War released the potential for new military forms that were
developing, demonstrated in the Falklands War, to become dominant. However, new Western wars would simultaneously be more
constrained by political, economic and media relations of global
surveillance, which bore increasingly on all actors in the new era
of warfare.

Segmented globality, diverse ways of war

The new mode of warfare is thus developing within this increasingly global society; it depends on and is simultaneously constrained by its other domains. Global power is not as even and fluid as the market model suggests: it is still hierarchically structured, unevenly developed, and extremely variably applied. The context of surveillance is common for all actors, but it is obvious that it works in different ways for different actors and in different wars. International institutions and law are highly dependent on the advanced West: this means not only that they are in some senses Western institutions and norms applied to non-Western states, but also that they have a particular critical potential vis-à-vis Western states. Likewise the West dominates global markets, but Western states that fight wars are expected to carry on delivering economic growth and prosperity and not to damage stock markets, while some non-Western states and armed movements are less subject to these pressures. Global media are still Western-dominated – although that is changing rapidly with the expansion of satellite broadcasting and the Internet in Asia and elsewhere. But Western states are particularly vulnerable in wars to adverse media coverage, and have to work harder than most to manage it successfully. (I shall discuss these implications further later when I come back to the new Western way of war.)

Thus global politics, markets and media are not undifferentiated wholes. Globality does not replace national contexts of power: on the contrary, globality is inconceivable without the numerous layers and segments, many of which are still nationally structured, through which it is constituted. The global world is a complex structure of overlapping local, national, international, transnational, regional and worldwide relations,[25] involving many different familial, community, ethnic, religious, cultural, professional and other networks. Obviously the many different protagonists in contemporary wars operate within the same general kinds of context, but each is located very differently within these structures and networks.

Hence, from their very different structural locations, different actors practise different *ways of war*. In table 3.3 I outline four

principal ways of war within global surveillance warfare: the
Western practised by the USA, the UK, France, etc. (discussed
further in the next chapter); the *national-militarist* practised by
established non-Western states such as Russia, China, India and
Pakistan; the *ethnic-nationalist* practised by new states and armed
movements – in the former Yugoslavia, many parts of Africa,
Indonesia and elsewhere – attempting to 'cleanse' the population
of territories they aim to control; and the *terrorist* practised both
by global Islamist groups linked like al-Qaeda and by national
movements like those in Palestine. Obviously, these four ways are
ideal types, not necessarily realized in any particular case, and
given states or armed movements may combine them in practice.[26]

Table 3.3 suggests many commonalities between apparently
diverse ways of war. Thus every armed actor mobilizes a political
base: whereas in total warfare mobilization was direct and often
totalitarian, in global warfare it is indirect and most often electoral. However, while electoral surveillance is a common con-
straint, its significance varies widely. Electoral contests are most
meaningful in established democracies. In many 'democratizing'
states, elites can still control media and other levers sufficiently to
more or less rig elections. Ethnic-nationalist elites even use violence to rig the electorate: by expelling other ethnic groups they
eliminate opposition and also intimidate their own group. Terrorists often don't operate as electoral actors themselves and mobilize their political bases through a combination of violent example
and ideological exhortation; but even they have proved alert to
mainstream electoral contests. And in many cases, following the
pioneering slogan of the Irish Republican Army/Sinn Fein – 'the
armalite *and* the ballot box' – they attempt to combine extra-
electoral violence with electoral activity.

In addition to electorates and other local political bases, all
kinds of armed actor are aware of *global* political and legal environments, in which many kinds of state and non-state actors are
at work, and which can impinge on their campaigns. All armed
actors mobilize global support: international opinion, transnational diasporas, and other extended global political bases. Particularly, all armed actors are aware of how their actions may be
perceived in global surveillance institutions: in the UN Security

Council and especially in Western capitals, in global and especially in Western mass media, in international legal bodies and by NGOs and others who attempt to enforce international law in war.

This global political environment is expressed largely through the common framework of *media surveillance*. Every armed actor targets particular sets of media, both those that particularly affect their own political base, and those that affect their enemies' support. For most actors, these are still primarily national media. In Western states, these are more or less genuinely plural and independent of the government, and have to be managed. In non-Western states, they are still often informally controlled by the government, and pressures can generally assure a classical 'patriotic' stance that Western governments can expect only from selected media (e.g., tabloid newspapers). But all actors are aware of the global media environment that feeds all local, regional and national media coverage. Stories and pictures move rapidly around the world, even if they are treated very differently in each regional and national media environment as well as by particular television and radio stations, newspapers and websites.

All types of armed actors also depend on a *political economy* that is more than national. Of course, the tax base remains the primary financial resource for both Western and established non-Western states: to this extent the national mobilization base of war finance remains intact. Many states also have national arms industries: indeed the number has increased markedly in recent years, and through marketing their weapons to other states and movements they aim to maintain their national military infrastructure. Thus the many new national arms industries have followed traditional great powers in seeking to supply the global market. Correspondingly global financing and global arms procurement have become increasingly important – and are not confined to ethnic nationalists or global terror networks. The USA financed the 1991 Gulf War partly through big subscriptions from two allies, Japan and Germany, which were disbarred from contributing militarily. It financed the 2003 Iraq War through a huge increase in government borrowing, lurching from Clinton's surplus into a massive new deficit. And both times it sought to recycle its investment by turning reconstruction into opportuni-

Table 3.3 Ways of war in global surveillance warfare

Global sources of surveillance	UN, states (especially Western), international law, global media, global civil society, global politics			
Global ways of war	Western	National-militarist	Ethnic-nationalist	Terrorist
Political base/ audience segment	national electorate, internationalized Western alliance/ public	national electorate	ethnically 'cleansed' national electorate, transnational diaspora	national, ethnic or religious, transnational diaspora or community
'Target' media segment/ management	national, global, plural	national-patriotic	national controlled	national, global
Weaponry	'precision' aerial bombing, artillery	aerial bombing, artillery	artillery, interpersonal killing, rape	bombing
Weapon platforms	missiles, tanks, integrated command systems	missiles, planes, tanks and armoured vehicles	tanks and armoured vehicles	civilian transport, human bodies (suicide)

	legitimate war?	degenerate war	genocide	genocide
Weapons procurement	national/international arms industries	national arms industries, global markets	global markets	global markets
Armed forces	professional	mass (mostly conscript)	conscript, gangs	movement/network
Ancillary arms	police, NGOs	police	police, parties	ethnic movements, religious networks
Combatant risk	avoided, transferred	accepted	accepted	embraced (suicide)
Civilian risk: massacres and denial	accepted: denied as 'accidental'	accepted: often intended, but denied	intended: 'cleansing', but denied	intended: atrocity embraced
Media-oriented action	'surgical' war as spectacle	traditional military success	'protecting' constituency	spectacular atrocity
Civil society/ anti-war	relatively strong	relatively weak	very weak	very weak

ties for US companies: the UK also sought to gain from its involvements. Moreover, Western and especially European arms industries have become increasingly internationalized.[27]

There are major differences between the four ways of war that I have identified. 'National-militarist' and 'ethnic-nationalist' states and forces often still fight according to a model of war based partly in total warfare. Their weapons are still classical mass-production rather than 'precision', their armies are still often conscript-based, they are not overly concerned about accepting combat casualties, and mostly they do not worry about causing civilian casualties – indeed they may even intend them in order to further ethnic 'cleansing'. However, ethnic-nationalist movements often depend heavily on diaspora funding, and even major states see themselves as representing transnational ethnicities (e.g., China vis-à-vis the Chinese across Asia). And global pressure inhibits non-Western elites, committed to integration into global markets and institutions, from waging all-out, extensively destructive wars against each other.[28] The damage caused to Iraq by Saddam Hussein's invasion of Kuwait and to Serbia by Milosevic's Kosovo venture is also a lesson for non-Western governments. And although civilians continue to be slaughtered in wars around the world, the examples of the Yugoslav and Rwandan tribunals and the trials of political and military leaders show that there could be costs. Many state, militia and gang leaders may not yet believe that these costs could apply to them: yet impunity can no longer be taken for granted. The global media and legal and political gaze is a part of every conflict. In many wars they play a considerable part, even if not always constructive: some limited interventions, such as the UN's Rwanda peace process of the early 1990s, may help provoke violence rather than contain it.

The 'terrorist' way of war is highly adapted to global surveillance warfare. Although 'terrorism' is such a politically saturated term as to be almost unusable, it has a rational core meaning: *a way of using violence designed to cause a political effect by creating terror and fear among a civilian population*. Of course, all forms of warfare inevitably create fear; civilian populations are always affected; and generating fear is often one of the purposes of action.[29] However, as a distinctive type of warfare, terrorism involves an *exclusive or principal reliance* on generating fear among civilians; this is the prime, rather than a secondary, rationale for the methods of action. As such, terrorism has always counted, for its effect, on the spread of knowledge of its violence. But the 'new' terrorist way of war has taken this to dramatic new lengths. There is often a shocking determination, otherwise shown today only in the cruellest episodes of genocidal killing, to maximize civilian casualties. This is combined with an equally strong embrace of martyrdom on the part of militants.

At a time when most armies are slowly following Western armed forces in becoming more casualty-averse, the positive commitment of terrorist organizations to their militants' deaths is very distinctive. The rationale for this way of war is directly connected to global (as well as local) media surveillance.[30] Suicide bombing is a measure not of the desperation of the youths who die, but of the extreme calculations of the armed movements that send them to their deaths. Its rationale is partly the symbolic nature of the embrace of death[31] – but also the instrumental fact that suicide killers can go where others can't and so create greater mountains of civilian dead in order to increase the media effect. 9/11 was a qualitative leap in terrorism, not only because of the numbers of victims,[32] but also because the attacks on the World Trade Center, the Pentagon and (probably) the White House were designed as atrocity spectaculars. The atrocities of flying passenger planes into skyscrapers were not only *for* the media, but also *of* the media – modelled directly on the disaster movies of the Hollywood that Islamists despised.

Massacre and denial in global warfare

The viability of this terrorist way of war underlines the obvious but disturbing reality that global surveillance does not simply constrain degeneracy in war, but in some ways may even encourage it. Global-era wars have not generally involved the catastrophic levels of killing that accompanied total war and genocide in the twentieth century. However, all ways of global warfare involve civilian massacre, the simultaneous killing of a large number of people. And one of the most important general laws of global warfare is that a massacre is the most media-worthy of events. All global ways of war involve massacres, but are envisaged in different ways.

In many non-Western ways of war, the killing and massacre of civilians are deliberate, in the sense of being openly adopted as a method and having a direct instrumentality. Thus terrorist bombings often intentionally target civilians, both because they are softer targets – easier to kill in large numbers than the better protected military – and because civilian atrocities are particularly shocking to media and publics. Thus terrorism involves the conscious exploitation of massacre. Because civilians are targeted as a means of attacking enemy states, terrorism is generally degenerate. However, in some cases terrorists also regard certain civilian groups, as such, as their enemies – thus their warfare crosses the line to genocide.

Likewise, ethnic-nationalist wars of 'cleansing' also deliberately target civilians in a genocidal way. While ethnic nationalists may be fighting simultaneous wars against armed enemies, their campaigns treat groups of civilians as specific enemies whose way of life is to be destroyed. In general, global-era ethno-nationalists don't aim to exterminate entire populations (in this sense the 1994 Rwanda events are an extreme and exceptional case), but endeavour to achieve the destruction of the enemy group primarily through their expulsion from their homeland. In this kind of genocide, massacre has a different function. It is mostly a means of terrorizing the population as a whole into accepting expulsion – a method of constructive flight. Contemporary genocidists value the publicity value of atrocity vis-à-vis their target population, but may often try to avoid global publicity for fear of international consequences and will try to explain away civilian killing as the accidental consequence of 'war'.[33]

Likewise, national-militarist campaigns are usually aimed at enemy states or armed movements. However, they often extend their attacks to the enemy's civilian population, in a classically degenerate way. Sporadic massacres intimidate the civilian supporters of the enemy state or movement. Like ethnic-nationalist movements, established states are keen to avoid global publicity and try to explain away civilian killing as the unfortunate consequence of war. Although ideal-typically we can distinguish ethnic-nationalist and national-militarist ways of war, in practice they may tend to converge.

Parties that practise civilian killing, even terrorists who openly embrace massacre, face the problem of accommodating it with global surveillance. Denial is always an issue for degenerate warriors and genocidists, but it has become more significant and more difficult with expanded global surveillance. They require developed denial strategies, combining factual denial with interpretative denial.[34] The most common interpretative strategy is to represent violence against civilians as simply war – either a legitimate method of war or an accidental excess. Unlike their predecessors, contemporary armed actors rarely have 'total' control over a territory or the option of simply blocking the global media gaze. Moreover, the terrorists' inversion of global norms is not as exceptional as it first seems. Global norms are generally built into the way that wars are fought, civilians are killed and denial is practised. The norm of democracy, for example, becomes an additional incentive to expel an ethnically undesirable population group: nationalists need a homogeneous electorate to achieve international legitimacy for their seizures of land. States readily apply the language of 'terrorism' to each and every armed opposition movement, if not to unarmed critics.

Western warfare shares the general tendency to produce massacres. However, it has a developed understanding of its own non-degeneracy: weapons are 'precise', civilian targets are systematically 'avoided', and deaths (let alone massacres) are 'accidental'. The question that arises is this: how plausible are the claims that the Western way has progressed from earlier degenerate warfare, and differs from the other contemporary ways of war? These are issues that I shall discuss in the next chapter.

Types of war, wars as imagined economies

So far I have tried to show how the general features of the global surveillance mode of warfare are manifested in the principal ways of war that have been adopted by different kinds of armed actor. It remains, however, to define how particular *wars* (episodes of warfighting) work. How do the relations and forms of global warfare, and the conflict of actors adopting different ways of fighting, manifest themselves in actual armed conflicts?

We can define a number of general types of war, actual and potential, based on the possibilities for conflict between actors using the different ways, as in table 3.4.[35] In general, the more classically interstate types, towards the top left-hand corner of the table, are for the most part increasingly avoided because of their potentially catastrophic effects. Wars between established non-Western states are increasingly rare, and these states fight mainly against secessionist 'new states', armed movements and terror networks. The wars that Western states fight are generally against third-tier, non-nuclear states, armed movements and terror networks.

In defining types of war, we need to recall that wars involve discursively constructed 'imaginaries'. All global ways of war involve 'economies of representation' in which not only 'threats' and 'enemies' but also the *means* of war are discursively shaped.[36] The main types of war are therefore constructed discursively by the protagonists: for example, the three main types of Western military campaign are represented by the ideas of war against 'rogue states', 'humanitarian intervention' and the 'war on terrorism'.[37] For those on the other sides of these wars, they are wars for 'national sovereignty' or 'holy wars' against Western imperialism. Indeed, 'national sovereignty' remains the fallback ideological position for 'national-militarist' states and 'ethnic-nationalist' campaigns. Table 3.4 presents a typology of wars schematically derived from how they are seen by different kinds of actor.

There are, however, 'imaginaries' of greater and less generality in global warfare. The most general imaginaries, for example the 'jihad' proclaimed by Osama bin Laden against the West and the Global War on Terror proclaimed by President George W. Bush, are *ideological frameworks* for their respective ways of war. They define good and evil, within which specific wars can be justified. The nature of these frameworks is loose and flexible, allowing for major strategic shifts, redefining the enemy and the course of action in line with specific political and tactical requirements. The Iraq War and its aftermath perfectly illustrate the flexibility in both doctrines: despite the long hostility between Saddam's

Table 3.4 A general typology of global-era wars

PROTAGONIST		ENEMIES					
		Western	National-militarist		Ethnic-nationalist	Terrorist	Civilian population
			Nuclear	Non-nuclear			
Western			*major global or regional war (potentially nuclear, avoided)*	international legitimacy vs. 'rogue state'	'humanitarian' intervention/war	'anti-terrorist' war	*not enemy as such:* 'accidental' massacre
National-militarist	Nuclear	'national sovereignty' major global or regional war (potentially nuclear, avoided)	'national sovereignty' major global or regional war (potentially nuclear, avoided)	'national sovereignty' secondary interstate war, regionally major	counter-insurgency	'anti-terrorist' war	enemy by extension: intended or 'accidental' massacre
	Non-nuclear	'national sovereignty' war	'national sovereignty' secondary interstate war, regionally major	'national sovereignty' secondary interstate war, regionally major	counter-insurgency	'anti-terrorist' war	enemy by extension: intended or 'accidental' massacre
Ethnic-nationalist		counter-intervention war	'national independence' war, ethnic 'cleansing'	'national independence' war, ethnic 'cleansing'	'national independence' war, ethnic 'cleansing'	'anti-terrorist' war	enemy as such: 'cleansing' and massacre
Terrorist		'holy war'	'holy war'	'holy war'	'holy war'		enemy as such: deliberate massacre

Ba'athism and bin Laden's Islamism, Bush was able to amalgamate Saddam into the general enemy of his War on Terror, while bin Laden's followers were able to ally with the underground Ba'athists against the American occupiers.

On the other hand, each particular campaign involves the specific imaginary. While general imaginaries are loose and flexible, specific imaginaries are of necessity much more focused and coherent. Neither the Islamist jihad nor the Global War on Terror has a precise objective or timescale: it would be very difficult to say when either was won, since the Islamists will never 'destroy' the USA nor, for that matter, will the USA 'destroy' a general phenomenon like 'terrorism'.[38] However, a specific war, such as the US campaign to overthrow Saddam or the 'resistance' war to expel the USA itself from Iraq, will necessarily have more coherent objectives; success and failure can be measured against them; rival actors can frame their responses in terms of how they will affect the originator of the campaign.

Thus it is the imaginary of a particular war that constitutes a better defined 'economy of representation', or an *imagined economy of war*. The party that initiates armed conflict is the primary definer, although it is always framed by longer political and cultural histories. Other actors may contribute to it, including not only the rival parties in the conflict, but unarmed actors: collective actors such as social movements and non-governmental organizations, and individual actors who are affected by the war. The imaginary world of a war constitutes an 'economy' because of the way that the actions of different actors are calibrated against each other, as I demonstrate in the case of Iraq in chapter 5.

4

Rules of Risk-Transfer War

How the West fights its wars, in conditions of global surveillance warfare, is all about risks. It is especially about managing relationships between political risks (to politicians) and life-risks (to combatants and civilians), to make each war a successful project – that is, to work as a risk economy. And the process of managing risks is all about transferring them – hence I finally name the new Western way of fighting 'risk-transfer war'. I shall come back to the general meaning of these propositions at the end of this chapter. First I want to demonstrate their significance in fifteen rules that govern how new Western wars work.

1   Wars must respond to plausible perceptions of risk to Western interests, norms and values

That wars must respond to threats might seem an obvious requirement for any war in any period. However, this is actually a specifically late-modern, Western perception. Historically rulers have often pursued wars to realize opportunities: now, although wars still open up opportunities for governments, it is no longer viable to present the resort to war in this light. The fundamental presumption of global surveillance is negative towards war and circumscribes its legitimate scope. In international law, wars can be fought only in self-defence or to uphold international peace and security under the authorization of the United Nations Security Council. In Western public opinion, the experience of twentieth-century wars – in Europe and Japan, of the Second World War, and in the USA, especially of Vietnam – has left people deeply suspicious of war. Global institutions and publics alike will best support, or at least tolerate, war in the light of manifest threats from states and armed actors. Certainly, the range of threats that are considered to justify armed response has expanded: national, common Western and global interests are considered closely inter-related; risks to civilians in war zones may be relevant as well as risks to more traditional state interests. But the idea that war is justified only as a response to a manifest threat is now deeply ingrained.

It is clear, moreover, that most new Western wars have not only been represented in this way, but have actually *been* reactive responses to aggression. Britain initiated its Falklands campaign in response to the Argentinian invasion; the USA initiated the Gulf War in response to the Iraqi invasion of Kuwait; NATO launched its Kosovo campaign in response to the Serbian war against the Albanian population; and the USA began the Global War on Terror in Afghanistan in response to 9/11. In every case except Kosovo, indeed, it has been sudden, shocking and (for political leaders) humiliating aggression that has precipitated the West's warlike response. This reactive context makes the idea of risk or threat instantly plausible, so that even those who do not support war can readily understand the need for some kind of response.

2 Wars must be limited in the risks they create for Western polities, economies and societies

If new Western wars must be comprehensible as responses to man-ifest risk, they must also not appear to create greater risks for Western society than those they are designed to address. The new way of war is built on the understanding that no war must ever again derail a government or political regime in the way that Vietnam damaged not just successive administrations, but the whole system of American power. Militarily, Vietnam had been a limited war for the USA, since it had never deployed anything near its full arsenal or manpower capacity: nuclear weapons were not used; North Vietnam was not invaded.[1] Political and socially, however, Vietnam had not been anything like limited enough. The problem was that the war had not been successfully isolated as a military struggle. Instead it had permeated politics and society, with profound, destabilizing consequences. Moreover, the escalating cost of the war had introduced an inflationary spiral that spread across the world economy, contributing to a general crisis of the Western system of power in the 1970s.

The lessons of this disaster reinforced an idea of limited war that was considerably *more* limited than ever before. If the West could not fight major or total wars,[2] it now saw that it could only fight lesser wars if they were contained in new ways. Above all war must be limited not just militarily and geopolitically, but in its domestic political, social and economic ramifications. The key understanding, therefore, was that warfighting must be carried on simultaneously with 'normal' economics, politics and social life in the West. It was imperative that it did not impact negatively on these. War should be a narrowly defined enterprise, for geopolitical and military goals that were achievable without wider disturbance. At best, war might even be a political and economic bonus; but the bottom line was that it must not damage polity, economy or society to any significant extent.

This new understanding of the context of war emphasized the fundamental change that had taken place in the evolution from total warfare. In the major wars of that era, Western governments could suspend many features of normal economic, political and social life, and insist that military imperatives overrode all others. They could nationalize firms, control production and direct labour. They could postpone elections. They could exert complete censorship over media. None of these things were possible in a limited war: on the contrary, if war spilled over into market economies, democratic electoral arenas and open media, this could have the disastrous effects seen during the Vietnam War. The elites' conclusion was that wars should be fought in ways that were calibrated with the economic, political and media demands that they faced. Above all, war should not risk the stability of the national economy, society or political system.

3   Wars are exercises in political risk-taking, therefore they must minimize electoral risks for governments and (if possible) maximize their gains

In total wars, democratic political elites did not separate their own from 'national' interests. In order to obtain complete control of their state, economic and media machines, elites often had to operate on a bipartisan basis, and trust that what was good 'for the nation' would also be good for themselves as parties and individuals.[3] In new Western wars, on the contrary, with 'normal' politics continuing, governments have remained partisan. Although they often appealed for and obtained a considerable degree of bipartisan support, governments' and leaders' own positions were much more pivotal to their wars. As we have seen they were often attempts to compensate for failures to pre-empt aggression. Above all, wars are exercises in political risk-taking: so any potentially adverse consequences for leaders and ruling parties must be contained, while potential gains should be maximized. Margaret Thatcher's Falklands campaign was an object lesson in how to 'cash in' military success, as her Conservative Party turned a very unpromising electoral situation into a crushing victory a year after the war. However, the Gulf War underlined the potential trickiness of such operations: despite the boost the war gave to President George Bush's popularity, he lost the subsequent election to Bill ('It's the economy, stupid') Clinton.

For political leaders, therefore, new Western wars must be calibrated not just with general economic, social and political stability, but also with the particular requirements of the electoral cycle. They seek the success of Thatcher, not the failure of Bush Senior. This means ever-closer attention to the timing of military actions: wars must not occur too close to elections, in case unpredicted difficulties appear damaging, but nor must they peak too soon, allowing the pay-offs of success to dissipate. The close connection of war with electoral politics is enormously complicated, of course, in the case of multilateral actions. In the Kosovo War, NATO's nineteen governments had to follow a single military path while managing nineteen electoral situations. In practice, the different political and electoral demands facing the many leaders meant that the war was tuned to the needs of the major players, the USA, the UK, France and Germany. Many governments could prevent the war from damaging them politically only by restricting their military participation.

4   Wars must anticipate the problems of global surveillance

Because electorates are almost exclusively national, Western governments still think largely of national surveillance. However, even this element of surveillance is mediated through the global and the international. National publics take notice of what allied governments and publics think, as well as of broader international official and public opinion. National media are influenced by global media. National politics and media are affected by norms of international legality and by decisions and judgements in international institutions. Although governments think in terms of accountability in a national public sphere, this is never autonomous to anything like the extent to which it was in the total war era. On the contrary, governments must always recognize how integrated global media, institutions and public opinion have become. Western nation-states are increasingly internationalized and, indeed, globalized.

Western governments need to pay much more constant attention than other armed actors to global surveillance. Their states stand at the centre of the global institutional networks: much more than others, they make and enforce the rules, and so they are expected to abide by them. Western public spheres are both more highly developed and more integrated than others: publics are better informed and have more diverse sources of information.[4] Civil society is more prominent, and the pronouncements of global non-governmental organizations have more impact on Western governments. Publics have been more sensitized against war by the experiences of the Second World War, Vietnam and the threat of nuclear destruction, and peace movements are a recurring feature of the political landscape. In the increasingly litigious societies of the West, no government can ignore the danger that international law could be applied against it. Hence the determination of the

United States government to exempt its officials and soldiers from the jurisdiction of the International Criminal Court through a system of treaties with its secondary allies (and despite the support of most West European states for the court). Despite such attempted legal fixes, global surveillance remains omnipresent, and all Western wars have to be prepared in this light.

5   Wars must be strictly time-limited: these are quick-fix wars

The cumulative effect of these constraints is that wars must be extremely limited in time and space. Limited war has been reborn as quick-fix war. None of the wars that I examined in chapter 1 lasted more than about three months, and the trend from the Falklands to the Gulf to Afghanistan and Iraq is actually towards shorter and shorter wars: from a little under three months to a little over three weeks. Kosovo bucked the trend and was longer than anticipated because NATO got it wrong, but even that war was over within three months from when the first bombs were dropped.

However, there is also a trick of representation involved in this idea of the quick war. The Falklands-Malvinas War, a classically interstate conflict, did indeed end completely when the British and Argentine militaries ceased fire. But in all other cases, war continued after 'the war' had ended:

- The Gulf War between the US-led coalition and Iraq (and with it the preceding Iraqi–Kuwaiti conflict) may have been ended by the first President Bush's ceasefire of 28 February 1991. But the Iraqi wars continued in the very bloody civil wars in southern and northern Iraq, and were followed by a twelve-year armed standoff between the USA–UK and Iraq, involving destructive UN sanctions, arms inspections, constant armed surveillance and intermittent bombing campaigns to 'contain' Iraq.
- In Kosovo, organized armed conflict ended with the Serbian-Yugoslav withdrawal, but sporadic political killings carried on, necessitating continued Western-UN military and political

presences (as indeed was the case in Bosnia-Herzegovina too). Moreover, war spread sideways into Macedonia and the Albanian districts of southern Serbia itself, necessitating a new Western military–political intervention in the former case.

• In Afghanistan, the war between the USA and the Afghan state ended quickly with the Taliban's dislodging from Kabul and the installation of a pro-American regime. However, the counter-insurgency war against the Taliban movement and al-Qaeda continues two years later and shows little sign of end.

And of course in Iraq in 2003, as we shall see in the next chapter, the devastatingly quick 'major combat' phase was succeeded by a protracted counter-insurgency war.

The success of the new Western way of war depends partly on its success in separating 'major' combat from other phases of war, and representing this alone as 'the war'. Western elites are well aware of the symbolic significance of closure: quick proclamations of 'victory' are needed to reassure publics and deflect media attention. The spectacular televised toppling of Saddam's statue in April 2003 – even before the Iraqi armed forces were completely defeated – represented an understanding that symbolically closing the war was as important as its military closure, and might even aid the latter. The corollary is that the counter-insurgency, peace enforcement and reconstruction phase is represented as radically different from war. Even if more soldiers and civilians are killed in this phase (as they certainly have been in Afghanistan and Iraq), counter-insurgency is not part of 'the war' that must be understood as already over.[5]

6   Wars must be limited spatially to distant zones of war

This separation is also evident in the spatial organization of new Western wars. It is paramount that real war is confined to war zones clearly separated from the Western heartlands in North America, Western Europe, Japan and Australasia. Only in this way, obviously, can the imperative to maintain 'normal' economic, political and social life in the heartlands be maintained. Real war must be something that goes on 'over there', just as it was for

Europeans in the days of empire, and for Americans even in the Second World War. Western military personnel may be sent into war zones, but they must also be extracted quickly from them. War mustn't touch the West physically – and hence economically, politically and socially – in any fundamental sense. Even (or especially) when, as in the Balkans, war zones are only tens of kilometres from the borders of Western states, maintaining this separation is crucial.

It might be thought that the Global War on Terror breaks down this separation. On the contrary, this is where the distinction between real, physical warfare and that which is symbolic, political and ideological becomes most crucial for Western governments. The great shock of the terrorist massacre in New York and Washington was that it attacked the assumption that real, physical war was 'elsewhere'. The priority of the US government was precisely to restore this separation. When George W. Bush proclaimed 'war' on terror, it was intended in two senses: *real war* in the war zones of Afghanistan, the Philippines, Iraq and elsewhere, and *policing and administrative action represented as war* in the Western heartlands of the USA and Europe. The representation of the latter as war was extraordinarily significant, but its difference from real war was also crucial. The imperative of 'war' – and the linkage to real war in war zones – greatly enhanced the campaign's ideological resonance and disciplinary effects. However, it was combined with the assurance that the campaign would protect American and Western citizens from real war. Bush wanted his electorate fearful and ideologically mobilized, but he still wanted the real violence against the 'terrorists' to be safely 'over there'.

Another dimension of spatial zoning in the Western way of war is the treatment of refugees. New wars, both between local actors and involving Western states, have produced refugees in increasing numbers: the global refugee population was estimated at 14.5 million in 2001.[6] Most displaced people remained within war zones themselves – many as 'internally displaced persons' who don't count in the refugee numbers[7] – or in the immediately adjacent states, which often became, as we have seen, 'bad neighbourhoods' by association. Western states strictly maintained this zoning, offering funds to governments or non-governmental agencies to support refugees in camps near war zones, while tightly controlling asylum-seeking in their own states. Thus the USA, the UK and France intervened in Kurdistan in 1991 to enable Kurds to return to their homes, rather than allow them to pour into Turkey, a key allied state. And after Milosevic's Serbia drove most of the Albanian population from Kosovo, European governments paid Macedonia and Albania to accommodate the refugees, allowing very few of them into Western states. Western governments' priority was to protect their own political and social stability – as much from the danger of exploitation by xenophobic parties as from the putative social disruption of the refugees themselves.

7 Wars must, above all, minimize casualties to Western troops

The 'risk-aversion' of new Western warfare has been widely noted. Preventing television pictures of 'body bags' was the central lesson learned from Vietnam. In a society whose members enjoy historically unprecedented longevity and personal security, loss of life has become increasingly difficult to justify and ideas of sacrifice have waned. In a society that has discreetly hidden even normal death, violent death is particularly shocking, and governments want to avoid its political costs. Soldiers are no longer conscripts[8] but relatively skilled professionals, in whose training governments have made investments; they demand occupational rights. They can no longer be treated as 'cannon fodder'. They accept the special risks of their profession, but they and their families will complain if their lives are unnecessarily or carelessly risked, and such complaints are likely to be magnified in the media and electoral politics. Legal and political campaigning by veterans is an increasingly common embarrassment for governments, and one they want to avoid.

Western governments are therefore profoundly sensitive to the potential political danger from losses of soldiers' lives. In most new wars, they have minimized casualties to levels that are tiny in historical terms: none of these wars have seen Western death tolls beyond the low hundreds. As we have seen, some may not even count as 'wars' by previous standards, and the Kosovo campaign took this trend to its limit by avoiding even a single Western combat death. Nevertheless, this risk-aversion must be contextualized and qualified. As we discussed in chapter 1, Western societies *will* tolerate loss of life, but they are less willing than before to tolerate futile loss. All hinges, therefore, on whether losses are perceived as justifiable. The problem of life-risk centres on how it is represented. There are three dimensions: whether the cause is seen as justifying loss of life; whether the war is seen as successful; and how actual casualty incidents are perceived. In a war that was strongly supported (for example, the first phase of the Global War on Terror in Afghanistan, viewed as a more or less direct response to 9/11), and seen as generally well run, the eventual deaths of soldiers were not problematic for US and Western public opinion. Conversely, in a war where legitimacy and strategy became more problematic, as in Iraq, deaths were less easy for publics to accept.

How these issues are played out depends on the media–politics nexus. It is not just a question of numbers, but of coverage, of representation and of political interpretation. Individual incidents, especially involving multiple deaths, may be more politically sensitive than steadily rising numbers. Shocking incidents provide visual hooks that enable dramatic coverage, critical commentary and political reaction – even if these may be expressed in terms of concern over numbers so as to avoid 'exploiting' particular deaths. News interest is (almost) all. In all Western wars, the numbers of wounded have been much greater than the numbers of killed, and the living wounded suffer over time, but their suffering is rarely so newsworthy as dead bodies dramatically produced.

The West's enemies often see its risk-aversion as an opportunity. Only impose sufficient casualties, they believe, and Western governments will retreat. From Saddam to Milosevic, they have tried to repeat the success of the North Vietnamese and the Vietcong. In some cases they have succeeded: the Somali warlord whose supporters killed eighteen American soldiers in 1993 and the Rwandan *génocidaires* who killed eleven Belgian UN peacekeepers in 1994 both forced Western withdrawals. However, in the West's 'wars', rather than its secondary interventions, they have not. The ruthless concentration of superior firepower has generally enabled Western states to prevail without casualties causing fundamental political damage.

8   Western forces should rely heavily on airpower and look to others – as far as possible – to take risks on the ground

Partly in order to minimize combat risks to its own forces, the West has relied more and more on airpower. Although in no case has this been sufficient on its own, it has played the central role in all new Western wars. In the Falklands, the Gulf, Kosovo and Afghanistan, extensive aerial bombardment preceded serious use of force on land (in Kosovo, of course, Western ground forces were not deployed at all until after combat was over). And to the extent that Western troops still take direct combat risks on the ground, special forces play an increasingly central role – except in the rare case of a major armoured assault, as in Iraq in 2003. Where extra Western personnel are needed in counter-insurgency operations, these are supplied to a growing extent by private 'security' firms.

   The risks of ground combat are transferred wherever possible to local allies in the zone of war. This is not always possible, of course: it was hardly an option in the Falklands-Malvinas War. And the West has not always seen the necessity: notoriously, the USA abandoned Iraq's Shi'ite and Kurdish insurgents in 1991, thus losing the main chance of an internal overthrow of Saddam Hussein. However, the West seems to have learned from this error: in all subsequent wars there has been a very significant role for local allies on the ground, while the West has provided the airpower and the overall direction of the war. The increasing interdependence between high-tech Western armour and relatively low-tech local armies has been seen in Bosnia-Herzegovina (the Croatian and Bosnian armies), Kosovo (the Kosovo Liberation Army), Afghanistan (the Northern Alliance–United Front) and Iraq (the Kurdish militia). These alliances have assisted Western states to avoid casualties to their own forces, and have effectively transferred a greater share of battle casualties to local forces. However, such transfers may bring military costs: as we saw in chapter 1, an overreliance on local allies was criticized for weakening the campaign to capture Osama bin Laden in Afghanistan. Moreover, local allies often fight much 'dirtier' wars than the West proclaims for itself: some Croatian, Bosnian and KLA commanders have been indicted for war crimes, and some Afghan warlords have become notorious for their atrocities against Taliban prisoners. In all cases alliances bring political complications, since local allies expect post-war paybacks from the West.

This role of local alliances should not be seen as an optional extra in new Western wars. As I stressed in chapter 3, Western military campaigns do not come out of the blue: they are nearly always interventions in ongoing political and military conflicts between local actors. While the West and the UN often represent themselves as impartial, neutral actors – and the discourse of 'humanitarian intervention' especially encourages such ideas – in reality it is inevitable that they take sides. When Western wars are responses to attacks on the West or its allies by particular regimes or movements, it is natural that the latter's local rivals (and victims) will look for alliance with the more powerful West.

9 The enemy must be killed: efficiently, quickly and discreetly

The other side of the West's own casualty-aversion is a determination to use force effectively to destroy the enemy's power and resistance. This does not always mean imposing large numbers of casualties: but it does mean a *willingness* to kill, even on a big scale when this is deemed necessary. And in contrast to total warfare, in which killing the enemy came to mean killing civilians, new Western war has brought a new concentration of firepower on the enemy military. In an ideal-typical (hence exceptional) case such as the Falklands War, it is only the enemy's soldiers who are killed. In general, it is only soldiers who are targeted as such, although civilians are killed in 'collateral damage'. Although civilian deaths remain highly problematic (as I discuss below), there is a consistent pattern in which more enemy combatants than civilians have been directly killed by military action (see table 1.1).

This more efficient targeting of weapons on the enemy could be interpreted as meaning that the West has reinvented war in a manner that escapes the degeneracy of earlier Western ways. It could also be seen as marking off the new Western way of war from other global-era ways of war that have in common (I suggested in chapter 3) the extensive, intentional targeting of civilians. In a historic sense, there is a transfer 'back' of the principal risks of being killed (as a direct consequence of military action) from enemy civilians towards the enemy military as such. This appears to reverse (for Western campaigns) the long twentieth-century trend towards overwhelmingly civilian casualties.

But before we examine these claims for Western superiority in relation to civilians, it is necessary to look further at the significance of 'killing the enemy'. In order to prosecute quick-fix war, the West needs to destroy the enemy's resistance quickly and effectively. It utilizes the most powerful, technologically enhanced weapons to devastate the opposing forces, blowing up their weaponry and vehicles and demoralizing their troops. (The 'non-lethal' weapons that are increasingly available have so far made little difference to Western campaigns.) Hence large numbers of enemy conscripts and fighters, with vastly inferior armour and often only lightly armed, have been industrially destroyed in new Western wars. Intensively and repetitively bombed, and even (in 1991) bulldozed into the sand, the West's enemies have reason to fear its military machine. Thus the new Western way of war is, in Victor Davis Hanson's terms (see chapter 2), far from a civilized way of fighting.

The virtual invisibility of the killing of enemy fighters gives credence to Baudrillard's idea that war has become purely virtual. The political significance of, on the one hand, the deaths of Western soldiers and, on the other, the killing of civilians obscures the ways in which enemy combatants are killed. The intensive bombing of Iraq and its army in 1991 killed, on any account, far more soldiers than civilians: but while the Saddam regime bussed journalists to view the civilian dead, it conspired with Western commanders to keep its dead soldiers unfilmed. The fate of Taliban fighters in Afghanistan similarly attracted little attention, although, given the numbers of civilians killed while the US attacked these fighters, the numbers of combatant dead must have been very considerable. Likewise over Iraq in 2003, all the attention has been on the civilian dead, although studies suggest more fighters have been killed. Combatants have come into the media picture mainly when they have been incarcerated. But however grim the imprisonment without trial suffered by irregular fighters captured by the USA in Afghanistan, it surely bore little comparison to the hell of being on the receiving end of aerial bombardment.

10   Risks of 'accidental' civilian casualties must be minimized, but small massacres must be regarded as inevitable

The history of modern warfare involves this paradox: while ideas of the distinction between combatants and non-combatants have become clearer, the practice of war has tended to harm non-combatants as never before. Legal protection for civilians has increased, but so has their targeting by armed forces as well as their general vulnerability. In the new Western way of war, for the first time, powerful modern states have developed a way of war that claims to address this contradiction. Western states have *not* regarded Iraqi, Afghan or Serbian civilians as part of the enemy state or military. On the contrary, they have repeatedly proclaimed that only regimes and armed forces are enemies. They aim to liberate civilian populations from oppressive regimes. Indeed, significant sections of the civilian population in the war zones have either been actively pro-Western (the Falkland Islanders, obviously; the Iraqi Kurds; Kosovo Albanians; some Afghans), or tacitly hoped for a Western victory (many Iraqi Shi'a; other Afghans; some Serbians and Montenegrins). Only some sections of the war-zone populations, often minorities (some Iraqi Sunnis, Pashtuns in Afghanistan and Serbs in Kosovo and Serbia) have consistently supported the West's enemies.

The political separation of 'civilians' from the enemy state or armed movement has informed targeting policies. Bombing and other force has been aimed at political and military targets, together with economic infrastructure deemed important to the enemy's military power. In the Falklands-Malvinas War, Britain pioneered a very precise focus on enemy military installations, eschewing attacks on the Argentine mainland. In the Gulf War, most of the bombing was directed at the Iraqi army and military and government structures and, given the intensive nature of the campaign, the number of direct civilian victims was relatively low. This gave rise to the myth of 'clean', 'surgical' war, although most of its bombs were not the new 'smart' weapons. Kosovo saw the most intensively monitored targeting ever, focused initially on Serbian forces and political–military installations, with accuracy down, in many cases, to individual buildings such as Milosevic's house in Belgrade. In Afghanistan, too, the USA claimed pinpoint targeting. Cities were bombed, but this was selective bombing with unprecedented accuracy, so that mostly only political and military targets were hit.

The problems with this idea of 'clean' war, apart from the slaughter of enemy combatants already discussed, were fourfold.

1   It was possible to separate civilians conceptually from the armed enemy, but practically this was much more difficult. Military installations were often in or near urban areas, and the targeting of 'regime' institutions, ministries and party buildings brought even more bombs into cities. However carefully the attacks were interpolated into complex urban areas, some civilians were bound to be killed or injured, because they worked in or lived adjacent to the attacked buildings.

2   Targeting errors, operational mistakes and technical malfunctions inevitably led to civilians being killed. Intelligence could be wholly or partially wrong: notorious cases in which civilians died include the bombings of the Amirya shelter in Baghdad in 1991 and the Chinese embassy in Belgrade. Bombing from 15,000 feet (nearly 5,000 metres), pilots inevitably made mistakes such as that which killed many Albanian refugees in a convoy in Kosovo. However 'smart' they were, missiles and bombs did not always work as intended: some inevitably hit the wrong buildings and people.

3   Many 'strategically' significant installations were, in reality, part of the civilian economy. Although the idea of strategic-only targeting implies a clear separation of military from non-military, 'strategic' was often understood to include economic infrastructure. The total war logic that converted not just munitions factories but railheads and electricity stations into military targets was not dead. In the Gulf War, attacks on 'dual-use' infrastructure (especially electricity, water and sewage systems) caused much larger numbers of civilians to fall ill and die after the war than died from bombs during the war. Controversial reclassification of some civilian institutions as 'military', as in the case of the attack on the Serbian TV

headquarters, brought more non-combatants into the firing line.

4   Although whole urban populations were not subject to indiscriminate area bombing, as in the Second World War, they were still comprehensively terrorized. Even if city dwellers believed in the general accuracy of the attacks, they nevertheless lived in fear of the inevitable errors, suffered the terrible, incessant noise of bombs and missiles falling around them, and in many cases saw the dead bodies of their fellow citizens.

Civilian deaths are therefore normal in new Western wars, and typically take the form of *small massacres*. Each of the West's wars has been marked by numerous such killings, most commonly of a handful of people, but in numerous cases of fifty to a hundred civilians at a time, with the largest single incident being the Amirya shelter bombing, in which around 400 died. Western massacres are indeed 'accidental' in the sense that they are not specifically intended and that efforts are made to avoid them. However, the risk of repeated small massacres of civilians is an understood feature of the way the West fights its wars. These risks are known and understood by Western military planners and programmed into the risk analysis of war.

The risk of massacres is also a completely predictable consequence of the other side of Western strategy and tactics, the protection of Western military personnel. Reliance on high-altitude and long-range bombardment keeps aircrew and soldiers safe; but it inevitably leads to errors of targeting and delivery that kill innocent non-combatants. So there is a *transfer* of life-risks from Western personnel to civilians, and this transfer is well understood by all concerned. In this sense, the 'minimizing' of risks to civilians is highly relative: these risks are not minimized as much as those of Western personnel, nor is their minimization an equal priority. To this extent, the consistent overall pattern of greater losses of life among civilians than among Western militaries is intended.

It is clear that the new Western way of war involves fewer civilian than enemy military casualties; fewer civilian casualties than in previous Western wars; genuine efforts to minimize these casualties; and more precise weapons that do improve the accuracy of targeting. In all these respects, the new way appears a historic advance on the degenerate Western wars of the total war era. However, it also clear that this way of war involves more civilian casualties than Western military casualties, and that there is a deliberate transfer of risks to civilians. In these respects, it is clear that Western war remains fundamentally degenerate. I shall examine the implications of this argument in the final chapter of the book.

11 Wars rely on 'precision' weaponry to sustain their legitimacy

The importance of technology is universally agreed. As we saw in chapter 2, many scholars have placed a technologically driven 'revolution in military affairs' at the heart of the changes in Western warfare. However, we have heeded Latham's counsel that the RMA is less a response to changes in technology than a cultural artefact of the new geopolitical and security environment and a new discourse of 'threats'. The discussion in this chapter suggests that a new political framework of war-making has defined the role of the new technologies.

The overriding characteristic of the new weaponry is precision, which has been well defined as 'the ability to locate high-value, time-sensitive fixed and mobile targets; to destroy them with a high degree of confidence; and to accomplish this within operationally and strategically significant time lines while minimising collateral damage, friendly fire casualties, and enemy counterstrikes.'[9] This definition captures not only precision's meaning but also much of its role in contemporary Western wars. However, this can be specified further.

- Militarily, more precise weapons make targets more tightly identifiable in time and space, so that they are easier to destroy and create less 'collateral damage'.
- Politically, more precise targeting helps accommodate the destruction within the tight political time-tabling and spatial zoning of the new Western wars.
- Ideologically, precision helps specify the crucial demarcations necessary to make possible the new way of war: between

warfare and 'normal' social life, between war zones and zones of peaceful commerce, between 'major combat' and aftermath, between enemies and civilians.

Claims of precision are particularly essential to all the ideas that sanitize war, masking its violence. Precision *defines* war, narrows it down, and makes it a discrete and manageable business. Precision makes war seem efficient in achieving delimited political goals, so that it does not intrude more than marginally and temporarily into Western society. Precision makes war *calculable*: it confirms that it is possible to weigh the political, military and human risks, produce a rational assessment, and act accordingly, with a realistic hope of agreement between project and outcome. Precision promises to make war like any other political, economic or social project. Precision subsumes the violence of war under its rational schema: it contains the bloody mess. The use of force is 'clean' and 'surgical'; only a few 'unfortunate' soldiers die; civilian victims are 'accidental'; and the enemy is 'defeated', its deaths hardly observed.

12   Suffering and death must be unseen: indirect, less visible and less quantifiable life-risks are more acceptable

Of course, war has not really been contained in this way. Enemy combatants have died, in large numbers. Civilian deaths were not isolated incidents: there has often been extensive suffering. Even among Western soldiers, there has been death, injury and trauma, even if there were also medical and psychological services to 'manage' them.

Moreover, wars did not end when Western leaders said they did. Often they continued long into 'extra time', and people continued to fight and kill long after the final whistle was blown. Reassuringly low figures for Western military deaths had often been capped at the official 'end' of fighting: in reality, Western soldiers continued to die after the 'war' had 'ended'. In Afghanistan, for example, almost all the US and Western deaths were after the capture of Kabul. Relatively low civilian casualty figures have also failed to count the much larger numbers who have died in the aftermath of the 'war' (see table 1.1). Further deaths, injuries and suffering have been caused

- 'accidentally' through continued violence between the West, its allies and its enemies;
- intentionally by enemies' deliberate attacks on civilian populations, sometimes in direct (Kosovo) or indirect (southern Iraq and Kurdistan, 1991) responses to Western military action;
- indirectly by unexploded ordnance – especially landmines and cluster bomblets – left by the West, its allies and its enemies;
- indirectly because of the destruction of basic services, such as electricity and water, particularly due to bombing;
- indirectly through the disruption of food supplies, especially in regions where a substantial proportion of the population was supported by humanitarian aid.

The significance of these categories of death and suffering has varied greatly between different new Western wars, but in all except the Falklands most of them have been present.

The bottom line is that indirect, less visible and less quantifiable casualties are more acceptable to the West than direct, visible and quantifiable ones. Where other causes of death are possible – enemy policies, civil war, drought, etc. – responsibility is less easy to pin down. Therefore the West finds the risks to civilians more acceptable and less decisive efforts may be made to minimize them. However, since the Kurdish refugee crisis after the Gulf War, Western leaders have understood that, where their responsibility can be established, even indirect casualties can rebound badly. Therefore awareness of these risks may lead to efforts to deflect political responsibility, as well as (sometimes) to real efforts to prevent harm.

13 Longer-term post-war risks must be spread as widely as possible through an international division of labour

Since Western campaigns always cause, directly or indirectly, considerable destruction of the built environment and upheaval in political and social institutions, as well as suffering and loss of life, they inevitably throw up problems of reconstruction. And since these campaigns are often fought in zones in which long local wars have left even greater legacies of destruction, the challenges of reconstruction, in the aftermath of Western wars, are often massive. Moreover, since new Western wars mostly intervene in pre-existing conflicts in the zone of war, they often do not fully resolve these conflicts. Instead, they alter the balance in them, in ways that threaten or lead to new violence. Wars premised on a quick fix increasingly turn out to require costly, long-drawn-out and complicated interventions to manage their aftermaths.

Here we can see that the conceptual distinction between 'war' and 'aftermath' is largely illusory. An 'exit strategy' is often seen as a *sine qua non* in launching a campaign or intervention: but often there is little scope for exit for extended periods. At best (as we saw above under rule 5), the end of major combat has led to a continuing conflict in which threats and covert violence replace all-out war. At worst, the 'war' that the West had 'won' gave way a different kind of war, either between local armed groups or involving the West itself. War 'endings' are therefore more about perception and management than they are about substance. The key is that Western publics *believe* the specific war to be over, even if they are aware that the Global War on Terror means that war in some more general sense has not gone away. Media must allow the war zone to slide down their running order; 'normal' politics and economics must swiftly return to the fore. In the war zone, airpower and artillery must give way to counter-insurgency and armed policing. The armed forces of the USA must increasingly give way to its allies', to police and civil servants from a wide range of Western states, to a UN-backed civilian administration, and to the many kinds of non-governmental organizations to which reconstruction tasks can be subcontracted.

The complex division of labour in Western wars becomes most apparent in this transition from 'the war' to 'the aftermath'. All major Western wars since 1991 have been US-led.[10] To advance 'common' Western interests in a belligerent way has always required US leadership and military resources. From the Gulf to Kosovo, Afghanistan and Iraq, there has been a consistent pattern in which the command, planes, tanks, artillery and munitions expended in the main combat phase have been overwhelmingly American. The UK and (usually) France have played key supporting roles, with lesser military contributions by other allies such as Italy, the Netherlands and Australia, and involvements, sometimes substantial but often token, by many other states.

US preponderance has usually been expressed in the organizational form of the 'coalition', preferred in every case except Kosovo. Coalitions allow the USA maximum flexibility in managing its wars, and especially the ability to shift gear rapidly and change roles in the 'aftermath'. In reconstruction, the UN, allies (even passive ones such as Japan) and the NGOs come into their own. Although the USA often prefers to keep a core of its own forces for 'stability operations', the division of labour involves it in handing over the tedious, long-term tasks of reconstruction – and maybe of counter-insurgency war – to its Western and local allies. The USA's exit strategy has hitherto been to load as much as possible of the long-term problems on to whoever else will take up the burden, including increasingly private 'security' companies, although there are signs after Iraq of a shift to accepting growing long-term loads. The theoretical exit strategy for the West as a whole is usually to hand over to a 'legitimate' local administration. But since local conflicts often continue to take armed forms, or threaten to do so in the case of Western withdrawal, the truth remains that often no exit is possible.

14   'Humanitarianism' and 'humanitarian' organizations must be annexed to compensate for violence against civilians

Increasingly Western concern for civilians has involved an attempt to compensate for the high explosive dropped on them – and the death, injury and suffering it causes – by adopting what is called a 'humanitarian' policy. Since the Kurdish refugee crisis after the Gulf War, Western leaders have understood that even indirect casualties can rebound badly, if their own responsibility can be established. Their new 'humanitarianism' is a way of addressing this problem.

Historically, the idea of humanitarianism had developed as neutral, non-belligerent aid for victims of armed conflict: the position adopted from its inception by the Red Cross, and still defended with intellectual coherence by Médecins Sans Frontières.[11] In the 1990s, however, as we saw in chapter 1, the label 'humanitarianism' was applied to armed intervention itself – where this intervention was supposedly motivated not simply by the self-interest of the intervening state but by some larger concern. This 'humanitarian' concern was variously to protect the delivery of humanitarian aid, to protect civilians from physical harm, or to further a 'just' political settlement: all of these, confusingly, were covered by this new use of the label.

The new Western 'humanitarianism' involves an attempt to co-opt traditional humanitarian ideas, action and organizations into the Western way of war. On the one hand, it reassures Western publics by promoting 'humanitarian' action *simultaneously* with the launch of war. Hence, from the start of the Afghan War, Tony Blair tried to insert a 'humanitarian' dimension, a position quickly embraced by George W. Bush, whose planes dropped food aid alongside bombs – however token and ineffectual this mode of delivery was. On the other hand, 'humanitarianism' is a way of mitigating, or appearing to mitigate, the *consequences* of war. Hence Western 'humanitarianism' becomes particularly important in the 'aftermath' phase. It has had real consequences: Western governments, international organizations and NGOs have provided genuine care for some of the injured and sick, and support for some healthcare and other systems – after the West's militaries have used the weapons that have harmed people and destroyed facilities. But their other, perhaps more important significance has been to reassure Western publics about the minimal, civilian-friendly character of the violence their armies have carried out.

15 Media management is essential: it maintains the narratives that explain the images of war

In the face of all these complicated demands, media management is utterly central to the new Western way of war – as recognized by most of the theorists whose work we discussed in chapter 2. Governments aim to produce a narrative that justifies what is being done, and to foster coverage that reinforces this narrative. Although governments can do much to promote their viewpoint positively, propaganda and control can no longer define coverage totally, as they did in total war. Instead, governments must rely on media picking up, reinforcing and, indeed, reinterpreting their narratives to get their case across. In the end, journalists must find government narratives more or less credible, and must not find reasons to depart fundamentally from them. And since journalism – as the name suggests – is a daily activity, daily events in the war must not cause too much of a problem for the official narrative or the media's own variants of it.

At bottom, wartime media management is less about promoting the official line than ensuring that events do not fundamentally disrupt it. Of course, many things happen in war which journalists and audiences find uncomfortable, and today's Western governments expect criticism and questioning. What they fear is a single incident that is so challenging that it threatens to 'break' the established narrative, suggesting to journalists, readers and viewers the need for a radically different understanding. It is often said that Western governments fear television pictures of deaths and atrocities: certainly they want no more of these than are unavoidable. They accept, however, that there will be some such pictures. Above all, they want to make sure that film is framed by the right kind of narrative. It is when the narratives go wrong that the pictures become insurmountable problems. Massacres lie, therefore, at the heart of the media management problem. Large numbers of Western civilian casualties in a single incident, such as 9/11 or the 2004 Madrid bombing, are probably the ultimate nightmare. Incidents in which significant numbers of Western soldiers are killed are also threatening, especially if the point of their deaths is clouded. Likewise the largest massacres of civilians in war zones threaten legitimacy. All such incidents have therefore been subjected to intensive 'spin', to reduce their political effects.

Although shocking individual massacres are most threatening, a *pattern* of violent events may also undermine pro-war narratives. The West's enemies understand this, as we have seen: hence the campaigns of attrition against Western forces in Afghanistan and Iraq. Casualty *numbers* are not so instantly dangerous, unless a particular figure gains wide currency and provides a hook for criticism. Hence persistent critics often try to popularize a rounded-up figure in the hope of crystallizing unease with the official narrative. Indeed opponents have increasingly made 'body counting' into a virtual industry, with the aim of making the totals count against Western policies. A significant aim of Western governments and militaries is to avoid any large casualty figures from gaining currency, and to contextualize the figures that are published in ways that render them less politically damaging.

Risk-transfer war and militarism

I suggested at the beginning of this chapter that the new Western way of war is ultimately about how risks are managed. We have now seen in the fifteen 'rules' something of how this is done. At the centre of the new way are the political risks that governments take: ultimately wars must not undermine, and should preferably strengthen, their domestic political and especially electoral situations. However, unlike other forms of policy-driven action, war mediates political risks via life-risks – to the West's own combatants, to enemy combatants, and to non-combatant civilians. In elaborating the rules, I have suggested that there are *systematic transfers of risk*, among which the following are central.

1   The physical risks of war for Western states are transferred from governments to their own militaries. This is, of course, normal in modern war and is not specific to the new Western way. However, unlike in earlier phases of modern war, governments make strenuous efforts to minimize these risks to their own soldiers and aircrew. These efforts have a crucial bearing on how risks are distributed among other actors.

2   In utilizing armed force in war zones, the West seeks to impose the major life-risks of its wars on enemy combatants, and to minimize those for civilians. Compared to earlier Western ways of war, this appears to transfer the burden of risk back from civilians to where it 'belongs', with the armed enemy.

3   However, in minimizing the risk to its own combatants, the West consistently adopts methods of war that effectively transfer risk from its own personnel to civilian non-combatants, so that far more civilians are killed, injured and otherwise harmed than Western military personnel. In any situation where the question of priority arises, the West is likely to put its own soldiers' lives before those of civilians.

In calling the new Western way 'risk-transfer war' I am making, therefore, three major claims about these systematic transfers of risk.

- Given the central priority of minimizing Western casualties, which in turn derives from the core media-political context within which governments fight war, these transfers are a large part of what the Western way of warfighting is now *about*.
- The transfers are understood, accepted and to that extent consciously *intended* by Western governments, military planners and the military operatives who carry them out.
- These transfers bare a fundamental contradiction between the norm of civilian protection and the reality of Western warfighting, and so make the *legitimacy* of this way of war fundamentally problematic.

Furthermore, 'risk-transfer' is a form of militarism as well as of war. By militarism, I mean a way in which war-preparations influence social relations in general.[12] Classical (total-war) militarism influenced society by mobilizing it (through conscription) directly into the army and into the war-industries and pro-war political organizations. New 'post-militarist' militarism does not mobilize directly, but only indirectly to achieve passive political support: it is measured in opinion-poll ratings for military ventures and for the leaders and parties that carry them out. In this sense, therefore, risk-transfer represents the influence of the form of militarism on the form of war. It is precisely because minimizing Western casualties is considered the bottom line of domestic political support that it becomes the *modus operandi* of war itself. Risk-transfer militarism operates through the media to neutralize electoral and other forms of surveillance that highlight the realities of death and suffering in Western wars.

War and risk theory

The idea of war as 'risky' is hardly new, of course. In any conflict, there is uncertainty deriving from the reciprocal action of two actors. But in many social conflicts, institutional and normative frameworks heavily circumscribe the area of unpredictability:

these are 'institutionalized risk environments', in Anthony Giddens's terminology.[13] The extreme role of uncertainty in war, compared to social conflict in general, derives from its violent character. Carl von Clausewitz long ago defined the clash of arms as unpredictable, with particularly open possibilities for expansion: 'there is no logical limit to an act of force.'[14] It followed that the rational political aims of states were subject to the play of chance; military command, Clausewitz concluded, was a craft rather than a science. However, strategic theory concerned itself with the risky character of the resort to war by governments and the adoption of particular strategic and tactical decisions by generals. It recognized, but took largely for granted, risks to soldiers' lives. It hardly recognized at all the risks for civilians.

The roles that soldier- and even civilian-protection play in the new Western way of war amount therefore to a radical *domestication* of war-risks as previously understood. The novel concern with saving soldiers' lives reflects the general taming of life-risks in modern society. In the West, where individuals are safer than ever from many of the historic dangers of hunger and disease, lives count more, and remaining risks are constantly assessed. Risk analysis, with its assumptions that risk can be calculated and weighed, has become universal. As Giddens puts it, 'A significant part of expert thinking and public discourse today is made up of *risk profiling* – analysing what, in the current state of knowledge and in current conditions, is the distribution of risks in given milieux of action.'[15]

This thinking has clearly invaded the military field. We do not know whether Western leaders have gone into wars with precise formulae for understanding the relationships between casualty numbers and opinion-poll ratings. But it is a reasonable assumption that, in most of the wars we have discussed, they have assumed that numbers of Western military casualties in the low hundreds, and of direct civilian victims in the low thousands, may be compatible with successful electoral feedback. Likewise it is reasonable to assume that they have weighed the electoral risks of massacre and found that, with prompt and effective media management, they may be contained.

However, Ulrich Beck – who famously described 'risk society' as 'an inescapable *structural* condition of advanced industrialization'[16] – has rightly criticized the 'mathematicized morality' of such exercises.[17] While policy-oriented risk assessment posited the manageability of risks, Beck and his sociological colleagues point out that 'even the most restrained and moderate-objectivist account of risk implications involves a hidden politics, ethics and morality.'[18] Risk 'is not reducible to the product of probability of occurrence multiplied with the intensity and scope of potential harm.'[19] Rather, it is a socially constructed phenomenon, in which some people have a greater capacity to define risks than others. Not all actors really benefit from reflexivity – only those with real scope to define their own risks. Risk exposure is replacing class as the principal inequality of modern society, because of how risk is reflexively defined by actors: 'In risk society *relations of definition* are to be conceived analogous to Marx's relations of production.'[20]

Surprisingly, sociological risk theorists have not generally paid much attention to risk in war.[21] Yet risk-transfer war hinges on extreme inequalities of definition. Western governments and commanders define risk for others, as well as themselves, differentially in ways that have dramatic consequences for whether people live or die. Beck pointed out that 'risks are related directly and indirectly to cultural definitions and standards of a tolerable and intolerable life.'[22] Western culture demands a high standard of soldier protection. It also demands higher standards of civilian protection than in the past, but in the end the lives of civilians – by virtue of their location in war zones as well as perceived cultural differences such as race and religion – are not as valuable as those of soldiers. And neither, in the end, is any more valuable than their political risk-significance allows.

Sociological risk theory has tended to emphasize the ways in which Western society has increasingly managed basic life-risks, replacing them with new, socially constructed risks. This discussion has suggested that Western warfare, in controlling life-risks for the military, not only defines but also *generates* new life-risks, which are only weakly managed, for civilians in war zones. Looking at global society as a risk society, it is difficult not to be impressed chiefly by gross inequalities of life-risks, and it is sobering to recognize these as artefacts of power.

5

Iraq: Risk Economy
of a War

In the risk-transfer way of war, each war is a discrete project that
generates its own economy of risk. In talking of a risk economy,
I use this term differently from those who see wars as 'economic'
arenas. They mean that wars are driven by market and corporate
imperatives and are reducible to commercial phenomena. If, however, a Western war is a political project, its political frame of
reference shapes market relations as much as they shape it. If relations between actors are defined by the definition of, exposure to,
and experiences of risk, then risk is the currency of Western wars.
But there are different kinds of risk: principally political risks
that leaders take, and life-risks to which combatants and non-
combatants are exposed. The crux of the risk economy is the commensurability of these types. Managing their nexus is crucial to
prosecuting a war successfully, and articulating it with the broader
political, economic and media demands of its time.

The risk economy of a war is above all an *imagined* economy.
The commensurability of political and life-risks, and indeed of one
set of political risks or life-risks with another, depends on how
people understand the linkages. Nevertheless, its effects are very
real: success or failure for politicians and generals, life or death for
many participants. Those who start the war set the terms of a war's
risk economy; they are also the primary risk-definers. However,
other actors also participate: these include not only armed enemies,
but also unarmed actors within the zone of war, in the West and in
the larger global environment: media, NGOs, social movements,
and individuals. Some are also exposed to and experience major
risks; yet those who are most influential in the risk economy and
those who are most exposed by it are manifestly not the same

people. Inequalities between risk-definers and the risk-exposed are central. Therefore a key question is: how important is the feedback from the risk-experience, especially of life-risks, for the course of the war and thus for the defining project?

In this chapter I shall examine these questions through the prism of the US–UK invasion and occupation of Iraq in 2003–4. This most recent, still ongoing, war has been the most ambitious to date, but its military and political success has been the most problematic of all new Western wars. And this is not just another case: success or failure in Iraq has general implications for the entire Global War on Terror and for the continuing viability of the new Western way of war.

Defining and imagining political risks

In preparing the invasion of Iraq, the Bush administration interpreted the first 'rule' of new Western war in a new way. There was no precipitating act of aggression by Saddam Hussein, and Bush acknowledged this by invoking two new doctrines. 'Pre-emptive war'[1] justified the USA attacking states perceived as likely to threaten in the future. 'Regime change' justified war to overthrow a governmental system considered dangerous to its own people as well as to the world. The idea of the 'war on terror' provided an overarching framework, linking the threat of Saddam to that from al-Qaeda and the recent history of 9/11.

Thus the manifest risk invoked to justify the Iraq War was significantly different from those of all previous wars. Certainly, Saddam had a record of violent aggression: externally against Iran, Kuwait and Israel, internally against Kurds, Shi'ia Muslims and Marsh Arabs. This history had led, after the 1991 Gulf War, to an ongoing conflict between the UN Security Council (in which the USA and the UK were the main protagonists) and Iraq. The UN attempted to enforce the arms control regime imposed on Iraq in 1991, while Saddam attempted to evade and obstruct this enforcement. The conflict led the UN to continue economic sanctions, which combined with Saddam's policies led to terrible impoverishment.[2] After the forced departure of UN weapons inspectors in 1998, the USA and the UK intensified military action

in the following year's Operation Desert Fox, and afterwards
enforced the 'no-fly zones' over northern and southern Iraq. Thus
the USA, the UK and the UN had consistently seen Iraq as an
international military danger, the threat of which needed to be
contained. It was clearly also a particularly brutal dictatorship, and
some of its violence was genocidal.[3] However, in 2001–2, many
believed that inspections, military action and sanctions had
worked. Colin Powell, the secretary of state, had said: 'We ought
to declare this a success. We have kept him contained, kept him
in this box.'[4]

Indeed the origins of the US attack lay in a perception of opportunity, not threat. Immediately after 9/11, Donald Rumsfeld, the
secretary of defense, had asked in the National Security Council:
'Why shouldn't we go against Iraq, not just al-Qaeda?'[5] The apparent successes of the campaign in Afghanistan emboldened the
administration to settle its scores with Baghdad. It was in this
context, then, that the USA raised again the question of Iraq's
development of illegal nuclear, chemical and biological weapons
('weapons of mass destruction' or 'WMDs'). UN resolutions on
WMDs constituted the only clearly legitimate international
grounds for action.[6] Yet presenting the WMD risk as urgent posed
a particular problem for Bush and even more for Blair. Certainly,
US public opinion had embraced the president's proclamation
of 'war' on terror and the campaign in Afghanistan. Voters were
familiar with the idea of the Iraqi regime as enemy and threat.
They were inclined to accept the president's amalgamation of the
Iraqi danger into the global terrorist threat, even if connections
between Saddam and al-Qaeda were lacking.[7] One poll showed
that 'Sixty-nine per cent of Americans said they thought it was at
least likely that [Saddam] Hussein was involved in the attacks
on the World Trade Center and the Pentagon.'[8] As Todd Gittlin
commented, 'there is some reason to believe that Americans'
knowledge of foreign affairs ranks low.'[9] With levels of ignorance
such as these, many gave Bush the benefit of the doubt, and even
sceptical Democrats were disinclined to oppose him. Nevertheless, there was public questioning and significant minorities
remained unconvinced.

Outside the USA, the task of convincing public opinion – and
governments – was altogether more difficult. Most worldwide

opinion and virtually all governments had shown great sympathy after 9/11. However, deep-rooted undercurrents of scepticism if not opposition towards US power were strong in many states, including those that were allies. Many governments, notably those of Japan, South Korea and Australia; in Western Europe, of Italy, Spain and Portugal; and in Central Europe, of Poland and other new NATO member-states, followed the UK in supporting the USA. But in most cases they were defying majority opinion against war: not surprisingly none would send troops to fight, although many later sent forces for peacekeeping and humanitarian assistance. But the governments of states such as France, Russia and China (permanent members of the Security Council), Germany (a rotating member in 2003) and many others took the opposite stance and openly defied the USA. The Security Council proved unwilling to accept the case for war.

Many have underlined the radicalism of the 'pre-emptive war' strategy. Michael Ignatieff, a supporter, argued that, 'In ordering troops to cross the Iraqi border, President Bush and Tony Blair have themselves crossed into the dark and unfamiliar terrain of the new world order created by 9/11, while their former allies and friends remain on the other side.'[10] For critics this was the problem: Paul Krugman saw it as an example of what happens 'when a stable political system is confronted with a "revolutionary power": a radical group that rejects the legitimacy of the system itself.'[11] He warned that the world should not underestimate its radicalism, determination and momentum. However, the opposite conclusion was also possible: the thinness of the war's ideological framework meant that Iraq was an unusually *risky* project for Bush and Blair.

The phoniness of the manifest objectives implied a high risk of failure in addressing them. 'This was a bold experiment', Joseph Cirincione commented. 'I tell my students . . . that they should take notes, watch one of the most radical political science experiments of all time play out. This is the first test of the idea that preventive war can stop proliferation. In order to do that . . . preventive war has to do two things: both eliminate the threat and deter others from pursuing this path.' Yet there was evidence that other potential nuclear 'regimes have drawn an opposite conclusion. . . . Officials in Pyongyang and Tehran may believe that if one day you find yourself opposed by the United States, you'd better have a nuclear weapon.'[12] Thus the war could increase the risk of the very proliferation it claimed to be preventing.

The wider international risks were considerable. As Polly Toynbee warned, UN backing mattered: 'Abandon even a weak international law and there is only anarchy: the price of an illegitimate US removal of Saddam would be free-for-all everywhere else.'[13] The US and the UK claimed legal authority for their actions under previous UN resolutions; but the fact that they had attempted, and failed, to get a second resolution that would have given them specific authority undermined their argument. Indeed it later emerged that the British government's legal advisors had been divided on the war's legality, and Richard Perle, then a member of the Pentagon's advisory board, conceded the illegality of the invasion: 'I think in this case international law stood in the way of doing the right thing.'[14]

Although Bush claimed to have 'saved' the UN from ineffectuality, many saw 'US unilateralism' in defiance of the Security Council (in reality, 'multilateralism *à la carte*', a coalition of the willing) as undermining it.[15] In an earlier study, I analysed how the cohesive Western bloc formed during the Cold War was developing in the post-Cold War era into a 'Western–global conglomerate of state power', spreading into increasingly global power networks involving most states.[16] The first phase of the Global War on Terrorism had led to a new, if regressive, extension of this global unity. However, the risks to these structures were such that Michael Mann asked, 'Will Shaw's "Western" and "global" states break apart under the pressures of American unilateralism?'[17] The answer was 'probably not',[18] but the USA was taking serious risks with global networks and institutions.

More profoundly risky was what Mann called 'global blow-back'.[19] Visions of regional conflagration in the Middle East, prevalent in neo-conservative writings as well as in leftist critiques of the 'new imperialism', were probably pessimistic. In the end, the USA might manage tensions like those between its Turkish and Iraqi Kurdish allies. But there was still much force in warnings that 'Those who think that US armed forces can complete a tidy war in Iraq, without the battle spreading beyond Iraq's borders, are likely to be mistaken.'[20] The most threatening blow-back, in the end, was al-Qaeda's growing threat: would the war actually stimulate the danger that the War on Terror was supposed to eliminate?

The radicalism of war for regime change made many fear a more difficult war, breaching the 'rules' that Western wars must be short, localized and with minimal effects on Western society. Alan Greenspan, chairman of the US Federal Reserve, warned: 'The heightening of geopolitical tensions has only added to the marked uncertainties that have piled up over the past three years, creating formidable barriers to new investment and thus to a resumption of vigorous expansion of overall economic activity.'[21] A respected British journalist reported that 'The prospect of war against Iraq has forced the Bank of England to prepare for the possibility of a long, bloody conflict that would lead to dearer energy, a crumbling of confidence, and a prolongation of the three-year bear market in equities.'[22] However, economic authorities probably wanted to believe in the US government's implicit promise of short war, and to avoid talking down the economy, so they may have held back from expressing fears of more serious risk.[23]

Critics tried to insert a deeper sense of risk into the debate, focusing mainly on 'unpredictable humanitarian consequences'.[24] A network of UN specialist agencies estimated that 500,000 people could 'require medical treatment to a greater or lesser degree as a result of direct or indirect injuries'; up to 100,000 civilians could be wounded; and another 400,000 could be hit by disease after the bombing of water and sewage facilities. According to the UN children's fund, 'The nutritional status of some 3.03 million people will be dire and they will require therapeutic feeding.' Iraq's urbanized population would suffer heavily: some 16 million depended on the monthly 'food basket' of basic goods such as rice, sugar, flour, and cooking oil, supplied for free by the government. Bombing would disrupt supplies and the UN would struggle to send in food from outside. The electricity network would be 'seriously degraded', leaving millions without proper drinking water because treatment plants would no longer function. Only 10 per cent of sewage pumping stations had generators, so bombing could provoke cholera and dysentery. At least 900,000 Iraqi refugees would go to Iran; another 2 million could be displaced inside the country; and 3.6 million people would need 'emergency shelter'.[25]

Medact, the UK affiliate of International Physicians for the Prevention of Nuclear War, estimated deaths could be five times higher than in 1991: 'The avowed US aim of regime change means any new conflict will be much more intense and destructive, and will involve more deadly weapons developed' since the Gulf War. The war could kill between 2,000 and 50,000 in Baghdad and between 1,200 and 30,000 on the southern and northern fronts in Basra, Kirkuk and Mosul.[26] Clearly, some of these risk assessments may have been little more than intelligent guesses, or on the high side, but they are all identified real concerns, reflecting the experiences of 1991 and other wars. However, some campaigners rounded the top end of these estimates to predict a 'worst-case' outcome, as in Amnesty International UK's rather sensational poster:

> War in Iraq
> 50,000 civilians dead?
> 500,000 civilians injured?
> 2,000,000 refugees and displaced people?
> 10,000,000 requiring humanitarian assistance?[27]

If it was theoretically possible that the invasion would lead to a prolonged war, in which these kinds of figures might have applied, that war would have departed fundamentally from the pattern of Western wars. Even thousands of civilians dead and tens of thousands injured, the more likely outcome, would represent a very serious result: there was no need to hype the consequences.

Some proponents of war recognized that, as Blair put it, 'If we remove Saddam by force, people will die and some will be innocent. And we must live with the consequences of our actions, even the unintended ones.' His moral case was that fewer would die than under Saddam's rule. When London saw its largest-ever demonstration on 15 February 2003,[28] Blair responded: 'as you watch your TV pictures of the march, ponder this: If there are 500,000 on that march, that is still less than the number of people whose deaths Saddam has been responsible for. If there are one million, that is still less than the number of people who died in the wars he started.'[29] This case was reinforced by the argument of an Iraqi exile that 'the Iraqi people have suffered so much at the hands of Saddam Hussein. They do not have the luxury of saying an unqualified "no" to war. . . . If Saddam stays in power, if he is let off another time, the damage would be enormous.'[30]

Thus the *trading* of numbers of victims was already the currency of debate. 'Risks' of allowing Saddam to continue in power and murder more citizens were traded against 'risks' of large numbers of civilian dead, injured and otherwise suffering as a result of war. An Iraqi 'would pay any price' to get rid of Saddam. Amnesty, in contrast, tried to show that the price could be enormous.[31] All these protagonists imagined a risk economy: one set of risks, to one set of lives, could be offset against another, to justify their preferred course. The logic of this economy led inexorably to trading numbers; individual experience disappeared. The 'price' that an Iraqi dissident was prepared to pay would probably be paid by others, who would not be asked if they wanted the deal; Blair didn't envisage himself as one of the 'unintended' victims; Amnesty's figures probably didn't help real victims, rather their inflation may have made it easier for politicians to dismiss concerns about casualties; and they certainly did nothing to help the victims of Saddam.

Did the risk economy imagined in these debates correspond to that in the minds of political leaders? As we have seen, those at the centre of the war-preparations faced other considerations, notably its electoral risks. It was widely recognized that George W. Bush wanted above all to avoid the fate of his father, whose presidency foundered after his first term despite military success. Bush and his campaign manager, Karl Rove, probably calculated that the Iraq War, like the War on Terror, would play well with the US electorate. War was timed to happen after the mid-term elections of November 2002, and well before the presidential vote of November 2004. They may have hoped that the disciplining effect of a national security crisis would pay off in the mid-terms – indeed it seemed to result in unprecedented single-party control of the presidency and both houses of Congress. Any difficult fall-out from the war could be dealt with in the eighteen months before the presidential election; by then it would be an achievement contributing to re-election.

For pro-war leaders in Europe the imperative was to minimize the electoral damage caused by their stance.[32] Silvio Berlusconi in Italy and José Maria Aznar in Spain appeared to avoid serious fall-out by not committing troops to the combat phase. Blair faced by far the most difficult task: as the USA's only major partner in the war, he faced a sceptical government, party, media and electorate. His stance neutralized the pro-US Conservative opposition but risked his own constituency. Indeed Blair's commitment to the increasingly thin risk ideology (WMDs and a Saddam–terrorism link) exposed him to acute political risk. Blair had come early to the conclusion that Bush was determined to wage war in Iraq and probably concluded in April 2002 that it was best for the UK to be 'onside', believing that thereby he would have more influence on how war was waged and presented.[33] In this way, he believed he could offset the risk: 'This was not a gamble, certainly not in its magnitude, that he had intended to take. He thought he could persuade the country of the case for war and found he couldn't. He calculated that he'd swing the public by securing a second UN resolution and didn't get one.'[34] In his manoeuvring between US hawks and sceptical British opinion, Blair repeatedly exposed his own position in both relationships, to the point where he became unsure of his own survival.[35] To critics, Blair's risk-taking was irresponsible: his own international development secretary, Clare Short, claimed just before fighting began: 'The whole atmosphere of the current situation is deeply reckless; reckless for the world, reckless for the undermining of the UN in this disorderly world, which is wider than Iraq, reckless with our government, reckless with his own future, position and place in history. It's extraordinarily reckless.'[36] However, if electoral risks constitute the 'bottom line' for politicians, this means that they are governed by the electoral cycle, and Blair also had considerable leeway: he probably aimed to hold the next British general election in 2005 and did not have to hold it until 2006.

Risk-exposure and risk-experience

For all Western governments in military action, the fundamental problem is to manage the political risks over the period dictated by the electoral cycle. In part, as we have already seen, this is a matter of fostering a more favourable perception of war-risks in the minds of voters. But risk in war is more than the currency of the abstract risks to groups that are traded in the imagined economies of political debate. It comprises also the concrete risks – risks to life, limb, health, social life and well-being – to which real people are exposed. However, what is crucial for the risk economy is not individual experiences of risk as such, but how these experiences are represented and fed back into the understanding of risk in the minds of policy-makers and electorates.

1 Western military personnel – the 'blood price'

Experiences of exposure to harm are universally understood in these representations as those of groups defined by their functions in war: Western combatants, civilian non-combatants, and enemy combatants. We have seen that much of the public debate prior to war turned on how risks to civilians were imagined – this was the priority of humanitarian NGOs, international organizations and protestors, and governments needed to respond to them. But the life-risks actually of greatest importance to the US and UK governments were those to military personnel. In Iraq, it was recognized, 'ground troops will have to be used and casualties accepted.'[37] A reporter asked

> whether one of the elements of the UK–US special relationship was whether 'Britain is prepared to send troops to commit themselves, to pay the blood price'. Tony Blair replied: 'Yes. What is important though is that at moments of crisis they [the USA] don't need to know simply that you are giving general expressions of support and sympathy. That is easy, frankly. They need to know, "Are you prepared to commit, are you prepared to be there when the shooting starts?"'[38]

However, Blair knew that it was vital that the 'blood price' should be as low as possible. This understanding drove two main types of policy: the adoption of military forces, strategies and tactics likely to minimize casualties; and the management of media coverage to minimize the political consequences of harm to troops.

Everything was designed to produce a 'swift and decisive campaign', so far as possible avoiding close confrontations in which soldiers' lives would be lost. Methods had developed from earlier wars: instead of 'softening' enemy ground forces with bombing first, or indeed substituting bombing for ground forces altogether, the new war was fought from the start both in the air and on the ground. However, this did not imply more US casualties. The aim was rapid, fluid advance, even at the risk of 'invasion lite'. Cities and towns were surrounded rather than assaulted; Iraqi forces were isolated and neutralized; the main body of US forces pressed up the motorway system, engaging only enough to secure its supply lines and capture key oilfields until it reached Baghdad. The assault on the capital was preceded by ferocious aerial bombardment and relied on long-range artillery in the few decisive encounters (e.g., the battle of the airport). Thus planning depended not on 'overwhelming force' but on 'overmatching power': 'attacking the enemy across such a spectrum of capabilities that his military would suffer systemic collapse.'[39] The new watchword, 'shock and awe', was often misinterpreted: it 'was never supposed to be about obliteration but about will power: stunning one's opponent into realising that your might was so enormous, so unbeatable, that the fight was as good as over. "The question is: how do you influence the will and perception of the enemy, to get them to behave how you want them to? So you focus on things that collapse their ability to resist."'[40]

In the advance towards Baghdad, there was of course serious resistance that (for about a week) created the appearance of an impasse. Murray and Scales describe the media response from the military point of view: 'Distressing to all was the reaction of the American media. Words like "stalemate" and "quagmire", along with dire references to Vietnam, were bandied about by commentators and reporters on the major networks.'[41] It was clear, therefore, that the political risks of even limited military blockages could be severe. No wonder then that the USA made a determined effort to create the appearance of victory, promoting symbolic gestures – such as the toppling of Saddam's statue – even before it had really established its control. Putting Iraqi radio and television off the air was very important in this effort. This strategy both created psychological pressure on the resisters and reinforced the idea of success in world media.

Changes to warfighting were adopted not only in order to save lives; they also enabled a more ambitious war to be fought with even less risk to Americans. This 'war' took under three weeks, from 20 March to 8 April 2003, by which time US forces were establishing their control in Baghdad and fighting was dying down. Casualty tolls were very acceptably low: only 117 US and 31 British military personnel died (not all of these due to hostile action). By the time Bush declared 'major combat' over, on 1 May, these tolls had risen to 139 and 33 respectively.[42] The war had been shorter and fewer US and UK troops had died than in 1991: success indeed, although Conetta put these numbers in a different perspective: 'In absolute terms, US, British, and Iraqi combatant fatalities were substantially fewer in the 2003 war than in the first Gulf War. Iraqi fatalities in 2003 were perhaps only 37 percent as numerous; US and British fatalities, 48 percent as numerous. Yet, measured against the numbers of troops engaged on both sides during the two wars, casualty *rates* were actually higher in 2003 for all concerned.'[43]

2   Civilians – the 'equation' with soldiers' lives

Hugo Slim has argued that 'What is so important in the American and British prosecution of the Iraq war is the obvious belief that there are such things as civilians in war, that they are like us and that it is wrong to kill them.'[44] Reports of US training emphasized that 'sparing the lives of the innocent whenever possible is a standard military doctrine and always on the agenda.' Soldiers were prepared to discriminate between combatants and civilians: 'To hone their reflexes, rapidly changing targets are placed in front of soldiers during training exercises. They must shoot at certain shapes and hold their fire at others. When troops storm wooden shacks in a mock village, gray silhouettes represent noncombatants and green ones the enemy.'[45] And yet we have seen in chapter 1 that previous Western military campaigns had harmed thousands of civilians, and in chapter 4 that this is understood as an unfortunate price that they had to pay. And there was reason to believe that Iraq could be worse: regime change would almost certainly mean troops forcing their way into the capital.

   Civilian risk-exposure was, of course, involuntary. Political leaders chose the risks that they faced. Soldiers made a bargain of risk-exposure when they signed up for the forces. Even journalists and NGO workers opted to enter war zones. But civilians faced risk just because they lived where they did and had relatively little protection. Politicians were highly protected on the rare occasions when they entered war zones. Soldiers (at least, Western soldiers) wore protective gear and were often inside armoured vehicles; they worked in organizations that looked after and aimed to protect them; they had weapons to respond to physical threat. Even journalists and NGO workers wore flak jackets and benefited from relatively well-resourced organizations that would airlift them out if risks became too great. Most civilians were directly vulnerable to any kind of firepower that happened their way, and were at the mercy too of failures of physical and social infrastructure. In many cases, the war moved so fast that civilians didn't have the chance to flee the sites of armed action; and when they did they often exposed themselves further.

Despite both general commitments and specific preparations to reduce the likelihood of civilian casualties, the USA and the UK used methods that would lead directly to them. Few doubted that bombing was very precise by historical standards, but the huge quantities of explosives inevitably caused many civilian deaths. The sympathetic 'Baghdad blogger', Salam Pax, wrote at an early stage of the attacks: 'Today before noon I went out with my cousin to take a look at the city. Two things. 1) the attacks are precise. 2) they are attacking targets which are just too close to civilian areas in Baghdad.'[46] Civilian buildings were frequently targeted in the belief that Saddam Hussein or his lieutenants were within. As reporters commented after a strike of this kind, 'It sounds surgical in theory. In practice, it still leaves a mess. Television pictures of weeping local residents suggested civilian casualties.'[47] On the ground, artillery bombardment sometimes had similar effects. However targeted, on Iraqi forces or on military and governmental installations, whenever (as they often were) these targets were in partially civilian areas, non-combatants were killed. Whenever US and UK forces encountered resistance and close-up engagement followed, civilians often got in the way. Fear of the coalition advance caused a 'frenetic' flight from Baghdad as thousands of citizens jammed the roads in taxis, cars and horse-drawn carts:

> The result was that Baghdad civilians were killed or injured as American forces and firepower swept through sectors of the city

and engaged Iraqi combatants. In one incident, at a south Baghdad interchange, two dozen civilian vehicles were inadvertently destroyed – their occupants torn apart or incinerated – by a US mechanized task force that was responding to an attack from nearby Fedayeen. Women and children were among the recognizable dead remaining in the wreckage days later.[48]

As the coalition tried to consolidate their control, protect their bases and begin to administer Iraq, attacks on their positions forced troops to respond quickly to potential threats. 'When you see something move, your first instinct is to kill it, but you can't', said one sergeant participating in urban warfare drills in the Kuwaiti desert before the war.[49] In practice, in several documented cases, US forces seem to have followed their first instinct; fearful of attack, they shot at innocent civilians, especially in cars.[50] Shootings of demonstrators also testified to the quickness of troops to identify civilians as potential military threats. Raids, in the search for enemy fighters and weapons, were another source of civilian deaths and could turn into massacres: 'Obsessed with capturing Saddam Hussein, American soldiers turned a botched raid on a house in the Mansur district of Baghdad . . . into a bloodbath, opening fire on scores of Iraqi civilians in a crowded street and killing up to 11, including two children, their mother and crippled father. At least one civilian car caught fire, cremating its occupants.'[51] In the guerrilla war, US forces, despite their claim to overall control, continued to use aerial attack and long-range bombardment. Attacking buildings believed to house resistance fighters, they sometimes imitated the 'controversial Israeli practice of destroying the houses of families of suicide bombers in the West Bank and Gaza' – previously denounced by the State Department.[52] At Fallujah in April 2004, no fewer than 600 people, including many civilians, may have died in a week of ferocious fighting to destroy the epicentre of the insurgency against US forces.[53]

A controversy about the effects of cluster bombs brought into the open the trade-off between soldiers' and civilians' riskexposures. General Richard Myers, chairman of the US Joint Chiefs of Staff, made a widely disputed claim that only one of the nearly 1,500 cluster bombs used by coalition forces had resulted in civilian casualties. John Humphreys put to Major-General Sir Patrick Cordingley, British commander in the 1991 war, the question 'How do you balance the equation there?' Agreeing that there was an 'equation', Cordingley replied that, while protecting civilians, 'At the same time we need to minimize the attrition against our own troops.'[54] And the British defence secretary, Geoffrey Hoon, explicitly invoked this equation to defend risks to civilians from cluster bombs: 'Balanced against that you really have got to face up to the issue of whether you are going to allow coalition forces to be put at risk because we do not use this particular capability.'[55]

3   Indirect risks – 'unseen' harm

The risks to which civilian non-combatants were exposed were not, of course, restricted to direct physical harm in the 'war' phase. Indeed cluster bomblets continued to cause damage long after they were used: Human Rights Watch reported that these munitions had 'killed or wounded more than 1,000 civilians' by the end of 2003.[56] Although the quick destruction of the Saddam regime eliminated the danger that it would attack its domestic enemies as in 1991, the war still did not end with 'major combat' but was continued in guerrilla fighting. In this war, guerrilla methods such as suicide bombing inevitably killed many civilians – indeed sometimes targeted Kurdish and Shi'a civilians as well as groups such as the new police. This risk had been understood beforehand: there were numerous warnings that a prolonged US occupation of Iraq would increase the danger of violent opposition to US forces.[57] However, civilians paid most of the cost of this failure, exacerbated by aggressive US counter-insurgency methods that also risked civilian lives.

Before the war, a US Army War College study had warned that the USA would 'also have to be prepared to undertake to provide time, considerable manpower, and money to the effort to reconstruct Iraq after the fighting is over. Otherwise, the success of military operations will be ephemeral, and the problems they were designed to eliminate could return or be replaced by new and more virulent difficulties.'[58] Indeed, 'Without an overwhelming effort to prepare for occupation, the United States may find itself in a radically different world over the next few years, a world in which the threat of Saddam Hussein looks like a pale shadow of new problems of America's own making.'[59] Later, when the administration's plans were becoming clearer, Marina Ottaway of the Carnegie Foundation put the point rather differently:

> The plan for post-invasion Iraq being aired by the Bush adminis-
> tration is a blueprint for occupation but not for political recon-
> struction. Unless the profound difference between occupation and
> political reconstruction is recognized early on, the United States
> will fail to leave behind a stable Iraq, let alone one that can serve
> as a model for other countries in the region. The price of chaos in
> Iraq, even if deprived of weapons of mass destruction, will be the
> continued threat of terrorism and regional instability.[60]

Despite these strong warnings, planning for 'major combat' was not matched by effective preparations for political and social reconstruction. The Iraqi state was administratively paralysed: all ministries apart from the oil ministry had been destroyed and the army and police were disbanded (a decision widely seen as a mistake when the USA had later to reconstruct these institutions, even calling on officers from the old forces to play key roles). Instability grew rapidly in the political, military and policing vacuums. The consequences were severe, except in Kurdistan, where there was little fighting and the autonomous administra-tion maintained stability. In the south and in many poorer districts of Baghdad, Shi'ite parties and militia moved to assert control, but their rivalries quickly spilled over into assassinations and violence.

The political vacuum and violence were accompanied by wide-spread lawlessness of all kinds. Early media coverage focused on the looting of the Iraqi National Museum, but this turned out to be exaggerated. However, looting was extensive: in Baghdad even the psychiatric hospital was attacked; the looting of seven nuclear facilities was another shocking case. Gang warfare was widely reported and caused many deaths. Murders, rapes and abductions of young women, carjackings and kidnappings were increasingly common, together with drug-related crime. As Robert Fisk put it, 'anarchic violence [was] now being embedded in Iraqi society in a way it never was under the genocidal Saddam.'[61] In this environment, people lived in fear and women especially were too scared to venture out.[62] But the US military did not have the resources to deal with a law and order problem that it had grossly underestimated.

For months after the war, public services failed to function and ordinary Iraqis experienced fundamental problems. As predicted, the provision of water and sanitation, electricity and medical supplies remained critical for many months in large areas of the country. Although widespread targeting of water, sanitation and electricity supplies has not been alleged (unlike in 1991), extensive damage was reported to facilities that were often in poor condition due to neglect during the 1990s. Many systems were not functioning at all, or only partially; and looting frequently compounded the problems. The shortage of drinking water was a problem across southern Iraq. Hospitals in many towns reported large numbers of diarrhoea cases: 70 per cent of children in Baghdad may have suffered.[63] In Basra, cholera was reported; however, a feared epidemic does not seem to have materialized. Health problems were often exacerbated because hospitals – already run down and lacking many essential supplies before the war – were damaged directly in the war or were looted.[64] In any case, hospitals in many areas were coping with an overload of wounded as well as the victims of these new post-war health crises. For a time, indeed, there was no big hospital fully functioning in Baghdad. Médecins Sans Frontières described 'many patients with chronic diseases who cannot get their medicines.'[65]

As we have seen, major indirect risks were foreseen by critics of the proposed war. Some of the worst fears seem to have been largely unfounded: thus the British Department for International Development was able to cite a Médecins Sans Frontières overview of the health situation: 'It is telling that after two weeks MsF has not found huge medical needs or a reason to describe this as a major humanitarian catastrophe in Iraq.'[66] Medact agreed that 'in the event food shortages were avoided due to stockpiling and the relatively short interruption to the OfF [Oil for Food programme].'[67] Likewise, the war 'caused no mass movement of refugees'; however, some thousands were temporarily displaced. Nevertheless, many civilians had indeed lost their lives or suffered injury, illness or other harm as an indirect result of the war. This was partly a consequence of the war as such: any rapid, violent campaign of this kind was bound to cause huge disruption. It was also a product of the widely acknowledged inadequacy of US planning for the aftermath. As Mann put it, emphasizing the weakness in the USA's overreliance on one type of power: 'The US went into this invasion with no credible plan for political reconstruction. Once again it was all military power, and no political.'[68]

Measuring the risk economy: the body counters

The statement by General Tommy Franks, US commander in Iraq, that 'We don't do body counts' has achieved iconic status among critics of the US campaign.[69] The words have been taken a little out of context: although assumed to refer to Iraq, the quote originated in Afghanistan in 2002, where Franks also had a command role. The full quote is, 'I don't believe you have heard me or anyone else in our leadership talk about the presence of 1,000 bodies out there, or in fact how many have been recovered. You know we don't do body counts.'[70] Franks's meaning may have been that the number of enemy casualties was no longer a measure of success, as the US military had understood it to be in Vietnam. However, it is easy to see why it should be taken as a reference to collecting figures as such: it is clearly true that the US–UK military and political leaderships are not keen to diffuse casualty figures for their own troops or (even less) for enemy fighters and civilians.

Certainly governments publish very precise information about individual casualties among their own soldiers. The US Department of Defense maintains a website that lists every single US death in Iraq.[71] The Ministry of Defence has a similar site listing British casualties.[72] These sites depend on the precise knowledge that military units – as highly disciplined bodies – have about the whereabouts and condition of their members. In historic wars in which soldiers' lives were more dispensable, modern armies may not always have known exactly which and how many of their men had been killed or wounded (although, even in the world wars, many produced quite good information). But in today's short, precisely controlled campaigns, with greater emphasis on the well-being of troops and the welfare of their families, they know for certain in almost every case. From the two sites, it is easy to compute very precise casualty figures, and a number of non-governmental sites provide this information, differentiating combat and other victims, and indicating the varying rates of attrition in phases of the campaign.[73] So while governments and the military 'do not do body counts', they have provided all the information necessary for others to produce very accurate and informative figures. Any Internet user can easily find them.

When it comes to civilians and enemy combatants, there is a very different picture. Official coalition sources may collect some pieces of information that would be required for accurate counts, but they do not appear to collect them all, systematically, in order to compute such figures even for their own purposes. Certainly they do not publish information in a way that would facilitate overall estimates, nor do they publish such estimates. Even figures that might be useful propaganda, such as the numbers of civilians killed by 'resistance' bombers, do not appear to be maintained. All this is unsurprising: in a campaign conducted with the aim of minimizing 'collateral damage' to civilians, any but the smallest numbers are likely to be unhelpful. Civilian death tolls in the thousands may be small by historical standards, but they have considerable potential to embarrass.

Accurate casualty figures are therefore difficult to establish. Civilians have been harmed in many different ways, but there are problems even in collecting information about specific incidents and areas of death and suffering. Civilians do not belong to disciplined organizations that can identify when they have been killed, wounded or become ill. In peacetime, hospitals and mortuaries routinely collect information; but many war victims did not come to hospitals, many of which in any case were damaged or so overwhelmed by the demands from the wounded and sick that they were unable to keep normal records. Information about violent incidents was collected and published by journalists, and about non-invasive harm by a variety of governmental and non-governmental agencies. However, this information was often erratically collected, poorly collated, and not systematized into generally comparable data.

It is worth asking, therefore, whether and why it is important to produce statistical information on casualties – and especially about the driver for *overall* figures. There is, of course, a relatively straightforward, basic rationale for quantifying war-deaths: war is fundamentally about killing in order to achieve political goals, and therefore it is very reasonable to want to gauge the extent to which it actually produces death. And since war is supposed to be about soldiers killing each other, the extent to which they kill non-combatants is clearly a matter of fundamental concern. The background assumption, however, is the belief that each individual life is of equal value: its loss is equally absolute in each case. As Iraq Body Count (IBC) has put it, 'Civilian casualties are the most unacceptable consequence of all wars. . . . each civilian death is a tragedy.'[74] Therefore each (but why only civilian?) life lost must be weighed equally, and summing up these equal individual losses will offer the best indication of a war's general effects. This procedure is then extended to injuries: similar overall figures are produced for those wounded in the campaign.[75] Interestingly, however, much less emphasis is given to injury in most statistical summaries, and even less in interpreting the effects of war. Clearly the death toll is the holy grail of casualty information.

Yet body-counting's driver is more than these obvious concerns. IBC expresses some of the extra motives: 'Adversities such as wars and civil wars threaten the survival and dignity of millions of people. The victims of these conflicts are primarily, if not almost exclusively, civilians – ordinary men and women.' But this claim is *not* so straightforwardly true of recent Western wars, in which commonly more enemy combatants have been killed than non-combatants, who are not targeted as such.[76] It is truer (in a body-counting sense) of wars such as those in former Yugoslavia and Africa where civilian populations are targets. IBC continues, 'Proponents of "modern" warfare also make much of the claim that their weapons are "smart" or "precision guided." Civilian deaths give the lie to such claims.'

The rationale is partly that body-counting is *easier* to do than other sorts of research: it can 'record single-mindedly and on a virtually real-time basis one key and immutable index of the fruits of war: the death toll of innocents.' While 'It is accepted that war causes many dire consequences for the civilian population even if

they are not directly killed or injured in military strikes. . . .
documenting and assigning responsibility for such effects requires
long-term "on the ground" resources. Immediate deaths and
injuries through military strikes can be pinpointed in place and
time, and responsibility straightforwardly attributed to the
weapon that caused the death or injury.' Body-counting is literally an attempt to make individual deaths count towards a critique of the war by adding them together:

> reports of incidents where civilians have been killed are scattered
> in different news sources and spread over time: one or two killed
> here, a few dozen there, with only major incidents . . . being guar-
> anteed *headline coverage*. But the smaller numbers *quickly add up*:
> and however many civilians are killed in the onslaught on Iraq, their
> death toll should not go unnoticed by those who are paying – in
> taxes – for their slaughter. It is to these all too easily disregarded
> victims of violence that Iraq Body Count is dedicated, and we are
> resolute that they, too, shall have their memorials.[77]

Thus the point of body-counting is that, by combining the
numbers of killed in 'minor' incidents, it gives them greater
weight, presumably (although this is not explicit) by giving them
the greater media coverage that is otherwise available only to
'major incidents'.

Not everyone who estimates civilian casualties shares all of
IBC's rationale. Carl Conetta of the Project on Defense Alternatives does not make an anti-war stance so explicit. Although 'significance for policy' is his prime concern, he argues that 'the
strategic significance of a casualty toll – its relevance to policy –
does not depend on achieving a single firm number or a zero
margin of error. In strategic terms, the difference between 11,000
and 15,000 fatalities (our approximate upper and lower limits [for
all Iraqi deaths, including combatants]) is only marginally significant. Whether the war's death toll registers at the upper or lower
end of this range, its repercussions would be about the same. In
other words: the achieved degree of precision is sufficient to use-
fully inform policy.'[78] However, this argument cuts across the
argument that 'each death is a tragedy', and they must all be made
to count. The novelist Gunther Grass expresses this viewpoint
clearly, as he makes his narrator say of the sinking of a ship carrying German refugees towards the end of the Second World War:

The numbers I am about to mention are not accurate. Everything will always be approximate. Besides, numbers don't say very much. The ones with lots of zeros can't be grasped. It's in their nature to contradict each other. Not only did the total number of people on board the *Gustloff* remain uncertain for many decades – it was somewhere between 6,600 and 10,600 – but the number of survivors also had to be corrected repeatedly: starting with 900 and finally set at 1,230. This raises the question, to which no answer can be hoped for: What does one life more or less count?[79]

So what is the point about numbers? Partly, it is that, in our rationalized, bureaucratized, democratized, global-surveillance world, what cannot be quantified seems less important. To 'count' in the sense of having weight, people (especially civilians, by definition 'ordinary' people) need to be 'counted' by number. The sense of the body-counting critics is that only when added up and totalled can the deaths of innocent victims weigh against Western wars. By showing that the outcome of war is more deaths than the ideology of 'precision weaponry' allows, body-counting can enter a countervailing entry in the bookkeeping of armed conflict. Body-counting aims to balance the 'equation' of war so that many civilian deaths count as much as the fewer military deaths that so clearly matter to the policy-makers. Body-counting is *an intervention in the risk-economy of war*, to make the risk-experience of civilians (and, for a few, enemy combatants too) as 'valuable' as the exposure of Western soldiers, and to make it significant for politicians, so that they in turn won't risk more wars of this kind.

Another novelist, Julian Barnes, has exposed the kinds of implicit weighting at work in the risk economy:

> there's another tacit calculation going on. The war depends on domestic public support. Public support depends in part on disguising the reality of war . . . and on calculating the acceptability of death. So what would be the best way of scoring the game? Someone, somewhere, some Machiavellian focus-grouper or damage statistician, is probably doing just this. Let's start with the basic unit: one dead Iraqi soldier, score one point. Two for a dead Republican Guard, three for Special Republican Guard or fedayeen. And so on up to the top of the regime: 5,000, let's say, for Chemical Ali; 7,500 for each of Saddam's sons; 10,000 for the tyrant himself. Now for the potentially demoralising downside.

One Iraqi civilian killed: if male, lose five points, female 10, a child 20. One coalition soldier killed: deduct 50 points. And then, worst of all (as it underlines the futility and hazard of war), one coalition soldier killed by friendly fire: deduct 100 points. On the other hand, gain 1,000 for each incident which a couple of years down the line can give rise to a feel-good Hollywood movie: witness 'Saving Private Lynch'.

'By this count', Barnes concluded (he was writing just at the end of 'major combat'), 'the war is a success. And television has more or less reflected the weighting of the above scoresheet: film a swaddled, bleeding, terrified child in hospital and airtime is guaranteed. With what blithe unconcern, too, it has disregarded the one-pointers.'[80]

Despite its difficulties, body-counting made impressive strides in the Iraq War. For all the efforts of media management, the presence of many journalists as well as officials of non-governmental organizations led to an unprecedented availability of information. Thanks to the Internet, this enabled 'virtually real-time' analysis of a depth and detail difficult to imagine in earlier periods, since it was possible to analyse quickly reports from very many sources. If Vietnam was the first 'television war', Kosovo and Afghanistan were the first 'Internet wars'. Modern body-counting, inspired by efforts during the Gulf War, really took off with these conflicts, but Iraq has been by far its most important test to date. Both Iraq Body Count's and Conetta's, the two most comprehensive out of a large number of studies,[81] are *indirect* projects that base their estimates entirely on these published press and media reports. As Bonini and Moulton's study of Afghanistan[82] showed, *direct* studies, based on community surveys on the ground, can produce significantly different findings that add to our knowledge – and increase the casualty tolls produced by indirect research. However, it is more difficult to make direct studies 'exhaustive and complete',[83] and those in Iraq have not yet offered overall findings on a par with these two indirect studies.

IBC's website gives constantly updated minimum and maximum figures for civilian deaths. By March 2004, this had risen to a range of 8,581–10,340, of which about 70 per cent had been in the 'major combat' phase.[84] In July 2003, IBC had also made an attempt to estimate civilian injuries: noting that, in the reports they analysed, 'the median injury – death ratio is 2.85, ... multiplying the maximum reported deaths ... by the median ... provides a figure of 21,976.' Extrapolating the roughly one-third death toll increase to March 2004 to injuries as well, as many as 30,000 could have been injured by the latter date according to IBC's methodology. However, as IBC recognized, injury figures raised considerably more difficulties even than death tolls.[85] IBC also provided a table of paramilitary attacks on Western targets (not including those in Afghanistan or Iraq) between 11 September 2001 and November 2003, showing a total of 3,375 deaths; they make the point that, 'For each civilian killed by "terrorists" on and since 9–11, the USA and its allies have brought about almost four non-combatant, civilian deaths in return.'[86]

In contrast, Conetta's analysis led to the conclusion that, in the 'war' phase (he does not go beyond this), 'between 10,800 and 15,100 Iraqis were killed, of whom between 3,200 and 4,300 were noncombatants – that is: civilians who did not take up arms.' Expressed in terms of their mid-points, his ranges (which allowed for uncertainties in the information) were:

Total Iraqi fatalities:	12,950 plus or minus 2,150 (16.5 per cent)
Iraqi non-combat fatalities:	3,750 plus or minus 550 (15 per cent)
Iraqi combatant fatalities:	9,200 plus or minus 1,600 (17.5 per cent)

Thus approximately 30 per cent of the war's fatalities may have been non-combatant civilians. Conetta also offered a critique of Iraq Body Count's study, explaining the difference between its mid-point total for civilian fatalities (during the period covered by his report) of 6,275 and his own 3,750. First, Conetta did not 'attempt to directly integrate casualty numbers from individual incidents as reported in the press. This, because we judged the problem of double-counting between the two data sources to be largely unresolvable. ... In our overall assessment, we concluded that the hospital and burial data was sufficiently strong and exten-sive to form the basis for an extrapolation that would capture all civilian fatalities.' Second, Conetta pointed out that 'The conventional concern with civilian casualties stems from the presumed status of civilians as noncombatants. But the noncombatant status of civilians cannot be simply assumed. In the Iraq war, militias and other combatants not in uniform played a major role.' He therefore excluded a proportion of 'civilian' casualties, as reported in hospitals, to account for un-uniformed combatants: 'In this sense, there is no direct comparison between our estimate and Bodycount's tally. However, if we take into account our average reduction factor for screening combatants – which is about 38 percent – the two tallies can be brought roughly into accord.'[87] Indeed the fact that Conetta included combatant casualties in his study was also an important corrective.[88] Barnes had suggested that media coverage had 'disregarded the one-pointers' such as the Iraqi military: IBC's disregard for combatant casualties mirrored this indifference.

Overall, Conetta offers the most sophisticated analyses and the most conservative figures.[89] His estimates may be qualified, as he acknowledged, in the light of later assessments: clearly more 'direct', on-the-ground studies may amplify his findings. Nevertheless, even from a critical perspective, it is better to under- than to overestimate. Conservative estimates that need to be revised upwards are more credible than overestimates that need to be reduced in the light of new information, since the latter could be represented as sensationalist. Yet Conetta interpreted his data in a radical way through comparison with the 1991 war: 'Looking at only the casualties incurred during the two wars', the overall casualties imposed on Iraq by Operation Iraqi Freedom were only 50 percent those of Desert Storm. However, 'the portion of war fatalities that were civilian noncombatants may have been twice as great . . . : almost 30 percent . . . versus almost 15 percent'; and at least as many if not more Iraqi non-combatants were killed, although the war lasted only twenty-five days compared to forty-two. These outcomes were due 'to the objective for which the war was fought: regime change. This dictated a much greater role (relatively speaking) for ground power and for combined arms warfare. And it dictated fighting in and near cities, producing at least two thousand noncombatant casualties in Baghdad alone. It also set the most demanding goal possible for ground forces and cast them into a conflict where the adversary's resistance was bound to be desperate.'[90] Thus, 'Although Operation Iraqi Freedom was supposed to exemplify the new warfare, it provides no unambiguous support for the hypothesis regarding civilian casualties. . . . the promise of a "low casualty" warfare will not be realized in practice if US strategic and operational objectives escalate in tandem with the advance of the new capabilities. Nor will the new warfare capabilities lead to an era of reduced conflict deaths if their promise serves as a rationale to wage more wars.'[91]

Risk rebound: life-risks and political risks

In the year after the overthrow of Saddam, there was increasing evidence that the political risks that Bush, Blair and their allies had *taken*, in going to war, were being exacerbated. Insurgency in Iraq was making life very difficult for the US occupation. As one commentator put it: 'With every atrocity, assurances of peace and progress ring more hollow as war and terror become part of the politics of re-election. The Bush administration is showing concern that the spiralling chaos of events in Iraq and Israel may damage the President's re-election bid.' The percentage of the public that called the war and its aftermath a success had dropped, leading some to believe 'that the centrepiece of the Bush administration – handling of national security, and the war in Iraq in particular', could now rebound on the president's re-electability.[92]

However, this situation had relatively little to do with quantifying the life-risks to which Iraqi civilians had been exposed.[93] It had everything to do, instead, with the risks to which the USA had exposed its *own* and other international troops in Iraq; the exposure of the thin ideological rationale of 'weapons of mass destruction'; and the counterproductive effects for the risks of terrorism that had framed the war. Only when all three factors had already done huge damage to the credibility of the war and the occupation did violence against Iraqi civilians become – over a year after the war – a serious media-political issue in the USA and UK. Even then the cumulative death toll was much less important than major *specific* incidents of harm: first the US assault on Fallujah in April 2004 caused widespread alarm, and then in May

2004 the exposure through photographs of abuse committed by US soldiers against Iraqi prisoners was the defining moment at which harm to Iraqis finally became a real issue. It was no accident that these questions became serious after the month (April 2004) in which more US soldiers had been killed than in any previous. Issues concerning Iraqi civilians acquired saliency because the occupation as a whole had gone critical. And it was *cruelty* rather than killing that in the end defined, in global media and politics, the violence of the occupation towards Iraqis.

This crisis was thus the culmination of a whole year in which guerrilla war had escalated, bringing, most crucially, a steadily rising tide of US military deaths. During 'major combat', relatively few military personnel had been killed or wounded. As US forces advanced through or flew over Iraq in their heavily armoured machines, they were at small risk from the outclassed Iraqi armed forces and other resistance. They were almost as much at risk from collisions, other accidents and 'friendly fire' mistakes.[94] Statistically, the risks in Iraq were so low that Mann could write: 'The new imperialists believe that the immensity and precision of their fire-power means that US soldiers do not *need* to be especially brave nor its citizens at all self-denying. This is a paradoxical form of militarism, accompanied by an ostensibly pacific culture which holds American lives truly sacred, not to be expended in wars or empire-building.'[95]

On the streets of Iraq, however, it may have looked rather different to US soldiers. Once they stepped out of their vehicles – or travelled in lightly armoured trucks or low-flying helicopters – they were far more vulnerable. The anti-occupation insurgents were quick to recognize this. By the autumn blowing up US soldiers was a daily occurrence. In November attacks shot down two US helicopters, in each case killing more than a dozen US troops. A year after the war was launched, the number of coalition personnel killed had risen from 148 to 665, of whom 565 were Americans, and the figures were rising fast. Nearly four times as many US personnel had been killed in the aftermath as in the 'war'.[96] These were the largest casualty figures of any US campaign since Vietnam. Even if they were low in any longer historical perspective, they represented real risks of harm for soldiers and others that the coalition deployed. The new vulnerability was reflected in the fact that, of all US military deaths, two-thirds, a higher proportion than in other wars, were attributable to hostile action.

These 'post-war' attacks proved a huge embarrassment to Bush, and prompted changes in both political and media management. The administration was already trying, with limited success, to internationalize the occupation, with greater involvement of the UN and of troops and police from allied countries such as Poland, Italy, Japan and South Korea. Now they sped up the process of 'Iraqification', with more rapid development of a new Iraqi government, and above all accelerated transfers of policing risks to hastily trained local troops and police. Bush must have hoped that, as one critic put it, 'the carnage in Iraq . . . can fade from the nation's consciousness over the course of 2004. There may continue to be deaths, but as long as American lives are not being lost, who cares? . . . The current deployment of 131,000 US troops could be cut in half and . . . those who are left behind will be largely confined to barracks, pretty much safe from the rocket attacks that are raising the military death count.' In this way it would be possible 'to hold the lid down on the boiling saucepan of Iraq long enough for Bush to be re-elected [in November 2004].'[97] Another way to spread the load was to employ private security companies: a year after the end of 'major combat' there were 20,000 mercenaries in Iraq, providing security for governmental agencies and training new Iraqi security forces, and sometimes embroiled in armed conflict.[98] The insurgents, while continuing to kill Americans, increasingly went for 'softer' targets. They blew up United Nations, Red Cross and Italian police bases with devastating results, and kidnapped and killed foreign civilians – journalists and aid workers as well as 'security' personnel.[99] They assassinated members of the Governing Council and caused spectacular massacres of Iraqi civilians: Kurdish party activists, Shi'a celebrating a religious festival banned under the former regime, and police recruits. Several of these attacks killed more than a hundred people – far bigger massacres than any the coalition forces suffered. A year after the war, more than 600 Iraqi policemen had been killed since the police re-formed, 50 per cent more than the number of US troops killed in the same period.[100] In addition, more civilians than troops were often killed in attacks on US forces: on IBC's figures (cited above), a total of 3,000 additional civilians may have been killed after a year of insurgency. And yet such incidents and figures did not cause as much direct harm to Bush's political standing as the smaller massacres of US forces. Moreover, in April 2004 the Shi'ite faction of Moqtada al-Sadr began a parallel uprising, so that the USA faced insurrection on two fronts. This raised the alarming spectre that Bush's political plan for Iraq, implicitly requiring the tacit support of the Shi'a majority, would unravel. The war would then require more rather than fewer US troops and involve long-term casualties. The spectre of Vietnam would not go away: Jay Letterman's high-profile US television show ended every programme with the names and photos of the many American dead, and controversy erupted over the Pentagon's banning of images of flag-draped military coffins, so redolent of Vietnam.

Furthermore, the precarious situation inside Iraq coincided with the increasing untenability of the ideological case for war. The evidence about Iraqi weapons of mass destruction had been at best circumstantial – based on knowledge of Iraqi programmes a decade earlier and uncertainty about subsequent developments – and one key argument was entirely hypothetical – the claim that, if Saddam's alleged WMDs fell into the hands of terrorists, they would represent an unprecedented threat.[101] There were explosive reports before the war that even the men charged with arguing the case internationally, Powell and the UK foreign secretary, Jack Straw, had strong doubts about it.[102] The British government had got into extraordinary difficulties over its dossier[103] on the case for war, first because of the revelation that part of it was taken almost word for word from a doctoral student's work available on the Internet, and later when a BBC journalist, Andrew Gilligan, alleged that it had 'sexed up' the security services' assessment of the risks of Iraqi WMDs. In discrediting Gilligan's allegation, the government enabled journalists to publish the name of his chief source, a Ministry of Defence expert, Dr David Kelly, who apparently committed suicide after his role became public.[104] This led in turn to a crisis of the government's credibility, which precipitated the setting up of a public inquiry, the Hutton Inquiry; but the report[105] was widely seen as 'whitewashing' the government. And although this damage to the British government mainly concerned *how* it made its case on Iraq, it fed on and sharply exposed underlying weaknesses in the substance of the case. The US administration seemed at first to be less exposed to risk rebound from its WMD assessments. However, President Bush had made very specific claims that 'the Iraqi regime . . . possesses and produces chemical and biological weapons. It is seeking nuclear weapons.'[106] Increasingly critical evaluations of the administration's pre-war risk assessments spread through US political circles, culminating in the resignation of David Kay, head of Bush's own Iraq Survey Group (which had replaced the UN inspectors), who announced that he no longer believed that Iraqi WMDs existed. Bush too was forced on to the defensive and obliged to establish an official inquiry into what had gone wrong.[107] In October 2004, the final report of the Iraq Survey Group definitively buried the idea that Saddam had possessed or was attempting to develop weapons of mass destruction.[108]

Finally, a potentially decisive element of risk rebound lay in the linkage with the 'war on terror'. In one respect, the occupation of Iraq ironically *created* the link between Saddam and terrorism that had been falsely alleged in the build-up to the war. In the aftermath of the US campaign, Iraq's borders opened and its internal policing evaporated. International groups that had not been able to operate in Saddam's Iraq moved in and joined Ba'athists attacking US and coalition forces. The Anwar-al-Islam group, expelled by US forces from their autonomous enclave in north-eastern Iraq, was reported to have regrouped in central Iraq and was held responsible for many atrocities. By late 2003 Iraq had a serious 'terrorist' problem that it did not have before the war.

However, it was global terrorist 'blow-back' beyond Iraq's borders that perhaps most seriously threatened the credibility of Bush's Iraq project. Coinciding with President Bush's controversial state visit to the United Kingdom in November 2003, a Turkish Islamist group linked to al-Qaeda caused two rounds of bomb outrages in Istanbul, Turkey's commercial centre, against synagogues and two British-linked facilities.[109] These attacks certainly provided Bush and Blair with support for the Saddam–terrorist amalgam, but they also suggested the alarming possibility that the war had given terrorists an increased incentive to strike at Western societies. And on 11 March 2004, exactly two and a half years after New York, al-Qaeda struck Madrid with devastating effect. In 'Europe's 9/11', seven synchronized bombs killed 202 people and injured more than 1,600. And, just as worryingly for Bush, Spain's ruling Popular Party, which had defied 90 per cent popular opposition to support the war, unexpectedly lost the general election held three days after the bombings.[110] Istanbul and Madrid were directly linked to Iraq through Osama bin Laden's public threats – reinforced by an al-Qaeda statement after Madrid – to Britain, Spain and other states that had supported the USA in the war. The atrocity raised the alarming prospect of repeated massacres of civilians in Western countries – attacks that would make voters blame governments rather support them.

As the 2004 US presidential election loomed closer, the risks that George W. Bush had taken in launching the Iraq War were already rebounding to a very significant extent. Although it remained likely that his formidable electoral machine would still save him, much of the political legacy of 9/11 had been squandered. A former Bush White House insider, Richard Clarke, published a devastating analysis[111] of how, before 9/11 itself, the Bush administration had neglected the terrorist threat in favour of its obsession with Saddam Hussein: 'what was urgent for them was Iraq. Al-Qaeda was not important to them.'[112] These charges were then taken up in the official commission of inquiry into 9/11. So it was not just this particular war that was in crisis: the Global War on Terror had proved far too flexible a framework, allowing the US administration to drag its people and many of its allies into an adventure that had actually exacerbated the real terrorist threat. At the same time, the Iraq crisis exposed deeper contradictions in the new Western way of war.

6

A Way of War in Crisis

The new Western way of war did not *require* the new grand narrative that spawned the Iraqi crisis. The new warfare had worked better in the Falklands and Gulf wars with limited, specific narratives about the crimes committed by the West's enemies, rooted in traditional ideas such as upholding sovereignty, self-determination and international law. However, 9/11 appeared to offer George W. Bush's right-wing US administration a golden opportunity to broaden the scope of the new warfare.[1] Bush's proclamation of the Global War on Terror opened up the first serious replacement for the Cold War narrative lost a decade before.[2] Now, once again, there was a generalized enemy, terrorism, on a par with communism. Once again it was possible to proclaim, 'You are either with us or with the enemy.'

The Global War on Terror appeared to have two great advantages over the earlier Cold War framework. Terrorism was inherently nebulous, so that fighting this enemy offered Western leaders great strategic and tactical flexibility; and the core enemy, al-Qaeda, did not possess the capacity to destroy the USA. Nevertheless, after 9/11 no one could doubt that terrorism in general and al-Qaeda in particular were serious threats. The Global War on Terror appeared to offer the US leadership huge possibilities to legitimate a wide range of operations and discipline its electorate, together with actual and potential allies. It appeared to offer a blank chequebook for repeated wars to Bush and his (initially rather less enthusiastic) military. This 'war' could pay off electorally and in global reach, and remain relatively low-risk.

However, the transformation of the new Western way of war into *permanent war* threatened to undermine the viability that had been developed over the previous two decades. The Global War on Terror had huge drawbacks, the flipsides of its strengths. Flexibility meant that Bush had no difficulty in defining Saddam Hussein's Iraq as part of the 'terrorist' threat, but the very transparency of this ideological stretching made it unsuccessful as a broad legitimation. Few governments and fewer publics were prepared to follow, the mega-coalition of 2001–2 quickly fell apart, and the military venture in Iraq became more difficult. And although terrorists might not be able comprehensively to destroy or defeat any Western state, their weapons were far more usable than the old USSR's nuclear warheads and a much more immediate danger to publics. The USA and Western Europe might shrug off new al-Qaeda-linked massacres in Indonesia and Turkey; but the 2004 Madrid bombings showed the trap into which the war was leading. Massive terrorist outrages in Western capitals could bring swift and devastating reaction against participating governments. Under the pressure of well-timed terrorist devices, electorates could be extremely volatile and quick to punish leaders they saw as deceitful.

So with al-Qaeda also signed up to the Global War narrative, the first rules of the new Western way of war would be broken. The risks to Western societies were becoming real and painful, and the electoral risks to governments threatened to follow. The need to fight 'terrorism' might frighten publics into backing permanent war – but it could also lead them to question war. Western wars could no longer be discrete, quick-fix military ventures confined to distant war zones. They would be long, messy, violent struggles threatening to turn Western cities into war zones. No longer would casualty numbers be minimal – on the contrary, larger numbers of military casualties would be compounded by the civilian victims of terrorist atrocities. This was a veritable crisis, not just of the Global War on Terror, but of the new Western way of war itself.

Militarisms of massacre

This crisis brought into focus the contrasting attitudes towards massacre, violence and cruelty in the Western and terrorist ways of war. The practitioners of the terrorist way of war not only intended their atrocities, in the full sense of aiming to achieve murderous results; they also openly embraced these results. On the other hand, Western warriors aimed to kill only combatants, and they took real measures to minimize civilian casualties; for them any such casualties were accidental and regrettable. The moral and political difference between the two could not, it seems, have been clearer. How was it then that the West often appeared to be losing the battle for legitimacy in global-era wars? The answer lay in the contrasting militarisms of massacre of the West and its enemies.

The murderous, even genocidal, logic of terrorist massacre clearly defied the basic moral standards of legitimate war, as understood not only in the Western tradition but also in Islam and other traditions. And yet this method of warfare was undeniably successful in mobilizing Muslims worldwide for Islamist causes, and even more in generating local and global support for oppressed groups such as the Palestinians. The first key to this apparent paradox was that this was an identity-based way of war: it justified its killings by often obliterating (according to its ideological convenience) the distinction of combatant and non-combatant, so that 'enemy' civilians were as much the enemy as any armed personnel. However, the second part was actually an equation of different civilian victims, justifying its own intentional killing of civilians by reference to the (however 'unintentional') killing of civilians by the West: 'If you don't stop your injustices, more and more blood will flow and these attacks will seem very small compared to what can occur in what you call terrorism.'[3] For the practitioners of this way of war, intentions were of little relevance: what mattered was that the West killed innocent members of their people. Deaths, whether accidental or intended, ended lives: and in the global media age they all added up to pictures of dead and mutilated bodies, which could be readily invoked by nationalist, Islamist and other ideologies to justify counter-killing. Thus were the 'accidental' civilian victims of Western bombing and counter-insurgency in Iraq, Afghanistan and elsewhere invoked by Osama bin Laden and others to justify their own more deliberate killing of Western civilians.

This terror-militarism had the virtue – for a mobilizing ideology – of being explicit in its embrace of violence, both for itself and its people and for its enemies. 'You love life and we love death', claimed al-Qaeda's video-statement after Madrid.[4] In contrast virtually all other ways of war involved much more extensive denial of the acts of violence they committed.[5] The new Western way of war, especially, with its deep risk-aversion for its own soldiers and citizens, claimed the ultimately impossible standard of 'clean' or at least 'cleaner' war. Its pretensions to civilian protection – however real in some limited senses – were easily represented as hypocritical. Its thousands of civilian victims spoke otherwise. In the counter-insurgency operation at Fallajuh, Iraq, in April 2004, US troops may have killed 600 local people in a week: far more than the victims of Madrid in the previous month. Many of the killed, to be sure, were combatants, who had taken up arms against the US occupation. But many were unarmed children and adults of all ages. Likewise, the deliberate cruelty inflicted by guards in US military prisons – at Guantanamo Bay and in Afghanistan as well as in Iraq – was so widespread as to represent something that seemed to have been officially condoned if not encouraged. No wonder that the Islamist equation was credible to many ordinary Muslims.

In global surveillance warfare, each armed protagonist and its civilian constituency weighed massacres, cruelty and body counts in the light of their own priorities. Western governments and electorates valued 'their' lives over those of others: killings of Western soldiers and civilians figured in their imaginations. But massacres and cruelty against civilians committed by the West were also authenticated by media coverage. The burgeoning regional television systems of non-Western parts of the world – notably stations such as al-Jazeera in the Middle East – conveyed scenes of carnage to wide publics and easily facilitated radically opposed narratives of violence. Images like the shocking photographs of US soldiers torturing prisoners went around the world. Politically, therefore, the West's militarism of massacre-concealment seemed weak in contrast to its enemies' militarism of massacre-embrace. The former might have worked in wars with conventional state enemies, such as the 1991 Gulf War: it had less purchase in the new conditions.

'Just-war' theory and risk-transfer war

One indication of the problems that the new Western way of war faced was the difficulty of providing a serious legitimation for it in terms of the West's own values and the global framework of law that they have informed. The principal moral tools that we had available derived from the 'just-war' tradition. As Richard Falk, a radical international scholar and critic of most Western wars, claimed, 'The "just war" doctrine provides the most flexible and relevant normative framework. It has roots in the ethics of all the great world religions, it is a vital source of modern international law governing the use of force and it focuses attention on the causes, means and ends of war.'[6] According to this tradition, as is well known, both ends and means had to be just, and most debate has focused on the problematic ends of some Western wars, especially in Iraq. However, the moral examination of a way of war raises the question of the means, or of *jus in bello*.

The new Western way appeared to address important concerns of this tradition. As Michael Walzer had pointed out in the major post-Vietnam restatement of this framework, it was axiomatic that the destruction of enemy is justified: ' "Soldiers are made to be killed," as Napoleon once said; that is why war is hell.'[7] There could be little argument then, it would seem, with the apparently sharper focus in the new way of war on killing the enemy. Of course, if killing could be shown to be superfluous to the goal of destroying the enemy's power, then its legitimacy would be put in question. Violence had to be proportional, not only to the goals of one's own side but also to the severity of the initial aggression. On first inspection, the intensive bombing of Taliban, al-Qaeda and Iraqi fighters fitted this bill, and the awesome weaponry used – such as the 'daisy-cutter' bombs – was merely an efficient means to this end. But if 'bombing worked' to defeat these enemies, it did so surely by slaughtering them. There were legitimate concerns about these victims. Since the slaughter in the trenches, we had learned to attach more significance to the lives of soldiers. When one side could minimize the risk to its own soldiers to very low levels, was it moral to practise industrial killing on a hapless enemy? Certainly, as we contemplated these inequalities of means, we might recall the slaughter inflicted on helpless office workers by terrorists using civilian airliners. But if the US's own killing was almost as one-sided, did the fact that Taliban soldiers or Iraqi insurgents were carrying guns make it so much more tolerable? Hanson's critique of '[t]hose who fight from afar, . . . kill[ing] "good" infantry with a frightening randomness and little risk to themselves',[8] would suggest that it did not.

If risk-transfer war raised questions for just war thinking even around the treatment of enemy soldiers, the issues concerning civilians went to the heart of the tradition. As Walzer had continued, 'even if we take our standpoint in hell, we can still say that *no one else* [i.e., other than soldiers] *is made to be killed*. This distinction is the basis of the rules of war.'[9] Walzer had also noted that the doctrine of 'double effect' provided a way in which 'it is permitted to perform an act likely to have evil consequences', such as the killing of innocent civilians. The key condition was that 'The good act is sufficiently good to compensate for the evil effect; it must be justified under [the] proportionality rule.'[10] This was little justification for the atom bomb on Hiroshima, although US apologists for this act have used a similar argument. However, it appeared plausible as an account of the 'accidental' killing of civilians in Afghanistan, Kosovo and Iraq, if only because the numbers of direct victims were much smaller and so the evil might conceivably be outweighed. And Walzer had perfected a rationale that has been widely applied in these instances: 'Double effect is defensible', he argued, 'only when the two outcomes are the product of a *double intention*: first that the "good" be achieved; second, that the foreseeable evil be reduced as far as possible.'[11] The latter is exactly what the West now routinely argued it was doing – with more plausibility than in the days before 'smarter' bombing – in its claims to be 'minimizing' civilian death.

However, Walzer had also pointed out a major problem for this argument when he pointed out that 'Simply not to intend the death of civilians is too easy. . . . What we look for in such cases is some sign of a positive commitment to save civilian lives. Civilians have a right to something more. And if saving civilian lives means risking soldiers' lives, that risk must be accepted.'[12] In risk-transfer war, this was precisely what was avoided at all costs. Aerial and artillery bombardments were undertaken in the firm knowledge that they would increase the risk to civilians compared to other possible means, military as well as non-military. High-altitude and long-range destruction was inherently indiscriminate.[13] Even UN peacekeepers were withdrawn when they were at risk: to save their own and other Westerners' lives, they abandoned civilians to genocidal terror.[14]

Surprisingly, Walzer had provided a way out for Western strategists in this situation. He immediately qualified his statement by arguing, 'But there is a limit to the risks that we require. These are, after all, unintended deaths and legitimate military operations, and the absolute rule against attacking civilians does not apply. War necessarily places civilians in danger; that is another aspect of its hellishness. We can only ask soldiers to minimise the dangers they impose.' Exactly how far they must go in doing this, he argued, 'is hard to say'; 'It is best . . . to say simply that civilians have a right that "due care" is taken.'[15] However, if this sort of escape clause made rough and ready sense in the context of wars where large numbers of Western soldiers were seriously risking their own lives, it was difficult to see how it might be sustained in the context of new Western wars such as those in Kosovo and Afghanistan where, after risk assessments have been carried out, only relatively small numbers of Western soldiers were risked.

The nub of the matter was that, as we have seen, the care taken for civilians was not only much *less* than the care taken for Western soldiers; it was *undermined* by a policy adopted to keep the latter safe. Risk to civilians was reduced not as far as practically possible, but as far as judged necessary to avoid adverse global media coverage. Civilians' risks were proportional not to the risks to soldiers, as Walzer had envisaged, but to the political risks of negative coverage. Thus even if there was a limit to the risks we could require of soldiers, Western forces in recent wars had gone nowhere near to this limit. Even if we could conclude that the aims of Western wars – including the 'war on terrorism' – were just, its methods were insufficiently so on the basis of established Western criteria.

Human rights and the illegitimacy of war

While this discussion confirms that risk-transfer war negates the criteria for just war, it has also revealed some of the problems of 'just-war' thinking in contemporary conditions. The 'flexibility' that Falk lauded had allowed Walzer to propose some very doubtful escape clauses. And the nature of risk-transfer war weakened the effect of traditional just-war reasoning: wars in which mortal risk to one's own combatants was reduced to very low levels, but dangerous risk was routinely inflicted on many more innocent civilians, required such flexibility that they extended the 'double effect' and 'proportionality' ideas to the point of absurdity. The problem was that, even if, *prima facie*, the new Western way of war met many of the historic demands for just war, it threw up a persistent problem of civilian death, injury and other harm that was morally objectionable as well as politically damaging.

The 'just-war' answer to this would be to change the way that the West fights its wars, so that the balance of risk between soldiers and civilians was changed. If commanders abandoned long-range and high-altitude bombardment, if they exposed soldiers to greater risk so as to save civilian lives, if governments and electorates were prepared to accept greater casualties among their own forces as the price of protecting innocents, if they instituted more rigorous regimes to prevent abuses of prisoners, then Western wars would be more just. To raise these demands, however, was to confront the scale of the problem: such a transformation would fly in the face of the core sociological realities of new Western warfare that we have discussed in this book. It was not clear that any Western government would, or even could, try to bring warfighting into concordance with the serious demands of just warfare.

By the established moral criteria, therefore, the new Western way of war is fundamentally flawed and likely to remain so. The degeneracy of Western warfighting did not end with total war and nuclear strategy: it has been reproduced in a new form. Indeed, the sociological conditions of the new warfare highlighted the depth of the difficulty. The concern to protect soldiers' lives led inexorably to the counter-argument for civilian protection. The *idea* of civilian protection, embraced by Western governments, militaries and publics – indeed sometimes the very rationale for war – led just as surely to ever-growing demands to put it into practice. These demands came mainly from human rights organizations on the liberal-left wing of public opinion, but they had a broad resonance and constantly threatened to gain, even if they didn't always achieve, real purchase in political debate.

The underlying truth of contemporary war is that, however good the rules for civilian protection, and however genuine the efforts of commanders to abide by them, it is not generally possible simultaneously to fight wars and protect civilian society in the zone of war. Britain's Falklands campaign, fought in the depopulated isolation of the South Atlantic, was the exception that proved the rule. Otherwise, new Western wars have been fought in populous regions with complex societies. Not only is it impossible to use powerful modern (even precision) weaponry without substantial killing of civilians. It is likely that even with the most scrupulous attempt to implement just-war principles – if it were politically viable – war would still cause much of the considerable harm that recent wars have done.

It is time to face the truth that war and civilian safety are not generally compatible. If Western society is to become really serious in its desire to save civilian life and well-being, it will have to move on from just-war thinking. That tradition has been designed, after all, to *enable* warfare, by indicating conditions in which killing might exceptionally be allowed.[16] And if we are not satisfied with just-war justifications, we may be applying different standards. War has long been protected in Western thought from the norms that apply elsewhere in social life; but we may now be applying to war the standards from which it has previously been exempt. 'Thou shalt not kill' has been tightened as a general norm, with fewer and fewer exceptions allowed; many Western states even decline to impose the death penalty. And yet war has remained a huge exception. Could it be that now that exception is being challenged, that tight norms against killing are being extended even into the realm of legitimate organized killing itself?

A serious concern with civilian protection derives, therefore, from ways of thinking that are very different from 'just war'. In particular, it arises from human rights thinking according to which all individual human beings enjoy the same claims to safety and freedom from violence. If we follow this line of thought, we cannot be indifferent to lives lost or damaged, however few they are by gross historical standards. Just-war ideas of 'proportionality' and 'double effect' – safeguards with an obvious potential for manipulation – have less relevance if we regard the rights to life and freedom from violence as fundamental.

In an age of human rights, the concern for individuals has been extended from Western soldiers to individual civilians, and even enemy soldiers too.[17] This concern was embedded in the rapidly developing raft of international law and legal institutions, which have been increasingly applied to actors in war. The International Criminal Tribunal for Former Yugoslavia (ICTY) provided a very significant model of impartial international justice, upholding the laws of war and genocide, albeit not without difficulties. Not surprisingly, the ICTY felt obliged to consider the case against NATO itself for its 'accidental' massacres of civilians in Serbia and Kosovo. The report of the committee it established made a case that there was no *prima facie* basis for formally investigating NATO's conduct of that war.[18] Whether, in terms of the current law of war, that was a correct conclusion is very arguable. But what *was* clear is that NATO *could* be held accountable, in principle at least, for the deaths of the civilian victims. What was driving the demand for justice was not so much the legal norms as the perception that all the individual lives mattered: the three people killed in the Chinese embassy, the sixteen killed in the Serbian television station, the seventy killed when a railway bridge was bombed, and so on. Incidents as small as traffic accidents, in terms of numbers of victims, could be matters for which the world's most powerful state could be brought to account, and in basically the same way.

Criminalization involved treating war like any other human activity, no longer *de facto* excluded from norms that apply in all other fields. Taking 'Thou shalt not kill' seriously did indeed threaten to make the practice of war very difficult. If the means of war were generally picked over with a fine toothcomb, in the courts, in the press and (indeed) in academia, then the legitimacy of war would be regularly undermined. As human rights conditions entered the governance of war, there was a fundamental threat to the very legitimacy of this institution. The laws of war were never really intended to be applied in criminal courts, and their enforcement threatened all warmaking. No wonder that the USA was so concerned about the establishment of the permanent International Criminal Court that came into existence in 2002.

But however much the USA resisted this drive, it stemmed from general trends towards intensified global legal regulation, heightened awareness of individual rights and extensive litigation – which derived much of their momentum from American society.

It is difficult, therefore, to resist the conclusion that the door has been fundamentally opened to new kinds of delegitimation of war. Regardless of Western governments' success in mobilizing media and public opinion in particular cases, the new Western way of war is generally vulnerable to new criticisms that are bound, sooner or later, to challenge its newly refined justifications. The failure of any of the transfers of risk could expose the West to risk rebound, and the risks of the new way of war would return to the West. In this process, it would be not just particular wars, but the way of war itself, that would be at stake.

Crisis of the new Western way of war

The crisis of the US–UK war in Iraq is therefore more than the failure of a particular war, administration or ideology, although it is all of these. It is also a crisis of the new Western way of war that has been developed over the last quarter-century, since the last great failure in Vietnam. And since this new way has been an attempt to reinvent legitimate warfare after the horrors of degenerate war in the twentieth century, the crisis takes us right back to fundamentals. Has warfare, as a way of pursuing valid political goals, returned to the dead-end that it reached in the period of the nuclear arms race? How fundamental is the failure of the new Western way and what are its longer-term consequences?

A lot depends, of course, on whether and how the crisis of the Iraqi occupation is resolved, and whether President Bush has been re-elected despite it: neither of these is clear at the time of writing. However, the failure has certainly been profound: for more than a year after the initial 'success' in toppling Saddam, the administration faced the mounting difficulties that were analysed in chapter 5. Even if the difficulties have been contained and Bush has been re-elected, Iraq is unlikely to be seen as a success. Much of the failure is due to the adventurism of the 'regime change' and 'pre-emptive war' ideas, and the looseness of the Global War on

Terror as a legitimating framework. As we have seen, it broke many of the 'rules' of new Western warfare that I outlined in chapter 4. To this extent the failure has been specific to Iraq, and it remains theoretically conceivable that the USA (or, in exceptional circumstances, Britain or France) could fight other more successful wars in the future.

However, any such 'optimistic' prospect for the new Western way of war evaporates once we consider the wider political fall-out. At the very least, the outcome in Iraq put Bush's re-election in jeopardy, and it distracted from and was counterproductive for the campaign against al-Qaeda. More than this, it demonstrated the political dangers of the laws of escalation and unpredictable consequences in war. The very idea that a war can be packaged as a discrete political project, managed successfully and brought to a tidy conclusion, has been dealt a massive blow. A fundamental question mark has been placed against the idea that, in today's global surveillance conditions, Western governments can use war effectively to achieve political ends. It must be doubtful if even Bush, if he has survived, will quickly repeat his adventure. Britain and other allies have surely had their fingers badly burned. To this extent, while it may still be too simple to say that Iraq is 'another Vietnam', the spectre is real. A whole way of fighting limited wars that was developed precisely to avoid Vietnams has become mired in something that has much of Vietnam about it. Many will learn anti-war lessons from this experience.

The chief lesson of Iraq is, however, that the future of Western warfare does not depend only on the decisions of the West itself. Western power has shown its vulnerability to guerrillas, militias and terrorists, even if it has been more successful against conventional enemies such as Saddam. The US failures in Iraq may embolden new enemies in other places. The West may not be able to choose, simply, to avoid wars; it may have wars thrust upon it. The worst danger is probably a sort of extensive (but less intensive) 'Israelization' of the West, or at least of the USA: immersion in many unending, unwinnable, if low-level wars and the corresponding brutalization of state and society. In this case even political withdrawal may not be enough to fend off further violence. The temptation for leaders such as Bush may be to go, as the Israeli regime has gone, down this road of permanent war. In this case, the 'rules' will change: although war would still be combined with 'normal' life, the permanent war situation will bring depressing new realities to Western societies. We have already glimpsed much of what this could mean in the first three years since 9/11. The failure in Iraq is perhaps the last opportunity to reassess the situation and avoid not so much another Vietnam as a global Palestine.

Alternatives to war?

The challenge is to accept the full logic of the value that Western society places on human life, and to seek alternatives to war. It is easy to dismiss pacifism as a naïve, utopian ideology that fails to recognize the realities of power and violence in the world. Certainly war has a long history in human society, and it is being renewed in many ways in the twenty-first century. Global surveillance warfare is integrated with many political and media conditions of global society. Whatever the West does, war will not simply or quickly disappear from today's world. Too many forces have too much to gain from it. However, the historical experience of the twentieth century was the degeneration of war into an indiscriminate slaughter, which engulfed societies. In this sense, I suggested two decades ago, we need a 'historical pacifism', which increasingly recognizes war as *in itself* a danger, to be avoided rather than chosen.[19]

Indeed the legitimate global order that was built after 1945 incorporated some of the lessons of this experience. It rested on a severe limitation of war, legally restricting it to national self-defence or under conditions of international authority. It also extended protection to civilians in war, codified genocide and developed the legal notion of crimes against humanity, and set up the UN Security Council as the ultimate authority in these matters. This structure assumed that war was no longer – if in strict law it had ever been – merely a *choice* of rulers. On the contrary it was a heavily circumscribed last resort in responding to aggression and threat. It was in defying this understanding that Bush broke the Western and international consensus over Iraq.

Faced with armed violence, it is tempting to respond in kind. It is easy to grasp the political force of Bush's declaration of 'war' on terror in response to what was indeed an 'act of war' by al-Qaeda. However, it is clear that the choice of war, here, was deeply mistaken and counterproductive: it gave credibility to the terrorist enemy, increased its support, and invited further attacks. The alternative was to claim the high ground of international law, to criminalize the enemy, and to make a different kind of global spectacle – one of global order in determined but non-violent pursuit of criminals. Bush could have invited the UN to establish a special international tribunal (since in 2001 the ICC was not yet operating) to oversee the global capture and trial of the perpetrators of 9/11. Likewise the UN could have established, at any time during the 1990s or early 2000s, a similar tribunal to try Saddam and his cohorts for their crimes of genocide. Law alone is not the whole answer: but it has great potential to delegitimize murderous rulers and leaders, and combined with a panoply of other coercive, non-violent measures it could achieve many of the results that are sought by war with fewer of the disastrous consequences.

It is certainly not possible, in our period, to exclude all armed elements from the exercise of global authority. Clearly a global legal campaign against al-Qaeda, instead of the Global War on Terror, would still have involved elements of armed policing: it would not have been possible to capture dangerously armed men without it. Clearly there are circumstances in which armed force should be used under UN auspices, if only to protect unarmed civilians who are menaced with genocide in places such as Srebrenica. In these circumstances the sort of guidance that the just-war tradition has provided, that soldiers must put the safety of innocents first, remains very relevant. However, these should be seen as exceptional, emergency actions, under the principle of avoiding war.

The crisis of the new Western way of war offers an opportunity, then, for Western and global society to reappraise the role of war itself in world society. It should be the beginning of the end of war.

Postscript

This book was completed six months before the 2004 US presidential election, in which George W. Bush was elected for a second term. As readers will expect (the foregoing chapters are exactly as originally written) his victory does not alter my judgement that the crisis of the Iraqi occupation threatened his presidency. This view is borne out by early evidence that suggests that Bush defeated John Kerry, his Democratic challenger, *despite* rather than because of Iraq. According to a nationwide exit poll, 73 per cent of those voters who thought 'Iraq' was the 'most important issue' in the election supported Kerry, against only 26 per cent for Bush. However, Iraq was the most important issue for only 15 per cent of those polled. On the other hand, 86 per cent of those who saw 'terrorism' as the most important issue supported the president, against 14 per cent for his opponent. Terrorism was most important for a slightly larger minority, 19 per cent.[1] These findings, particularly significant because based on interviews at the time of voting, express very graphically the distinction between the Global War on Terror and the real war in Iraq that I have emphasized in the preceding chapters. The GWoT as an ideological framework played well for Bush; many more voters than those who bought terrorism as the principal issue may have been swayed by his 'strong' stance, tied to his simplistic emphasis on 'moral values' that was endorsed as the main issue by even more of his supporters.

Bush's 'terrorism' theme was handily reinforced by Osama bin Laden, who popped up in a video released just four days before polling. The symbiosis was striking: while bin Laden could not resist using the US election to underline his credibility in the

Muslim world, so too the visible reminder of his continued threat was a godsend to Bush. A video was exactly what he needed for the TV networks – so much less threatening electorally than a Madrid-style pre-election attack. And just as the pseudo-war on terror had, from the start, legitimated Bush's risky adventure in regime change, so now it distracted attention from the real, messy war that daily cost the lives of US soldiers and civilians in Iraq. Although the preparations for a major new onslaught on the 'resistance' stronghold of Fallujah were well advertised, the administration prudently delayed its commencement until after the election. Within days of Bush's victory, fierce bombing and house-to-house fighting had cleared the city, with casualties reported to be greater than in the first attack of April 2004. US casualties have brought their overall death toll attributed to hostile action to over 1,000 at the time of writing, out of nearly 1,300 US dead.

In the aftermath of the election, many emphasized that Bush, now a second-term incumbent, had been freed from electoral constraints to pursue his ideological agenda unencumbered.[2] New military ventures seemed on the cards. Yet too many US troops were likely to remain tied down in Iraq, and despite Bush's electoral survival the costs of the war, politically as well as financially, seemed likely to have given even the most triumphant president and his advisors food for thought. It was clear that none of his major international allies had an appetite for further wars, as Britain joined France and Germany in efforts to keep communication open with another member of the 'axis of evil', Iran, believed by Bush to be developing nuclear weapons, while discussions with the third member, North Korea, were also ongoing. While Bush consolidated his grip on the administration, losing the 'moderating' influence of Colin Powell, it was too early to say that Iraq was the last major war of his presidency, but it was not too soon to hope.

Moreover, evidence of the costs of the Iraq War to its people has grown. Five US scientists published a striking study in *The Lancet* that estimated 98,000 more deaths than expected from normal mortality in Iraq between early 2002 and late 2004.[3] Based on a household survey – we saw from Afghanistan that this method could produce higher casualty numbers – this proposed a figure almost an order higher than the 14,000 to 16,000 estimated at that time by Iraq Body Count from media reports, which itself could be subjected to Conetta's reservations about combatants among the civilian casualties. Nevertheless, despite the inevitable problems of such a study,[4] its methodology appeared relatively robust. Notwithstanding 'wide uncertainty' about the overall estimate – the range at the 95 per cent confidence interval was 8,000 to 194,000 – a reviewer concluded that 'the sample data are, however, more comfortably consistent with realities closer to the centre than outer limits of the associated confidence interval.'[5] Moving towards a conclusion that many tens of thousands of civilians had probably died in Iraq certainly shifted the debate, producing pressure for the British government to commission comprehensive research. As the authors of the article in *The Lancet* commented, 'This survey shows that with modest funds, four weeks, and seven Iraqi team members willing to risk their lives, a useful measure of civilian deaths could be obtained. There seems to be little excuse for occupying forces to not be able to provide more precise tallies.'[6] A Count the Casualties Campaign was launched[7] and Tony Blair himself felt the need to respond, although rejecting the need for an independent study. This renewed debate has not changed my own view that, by themselves, casualty numbers, however shocking, will not achieve a decisive shift in the political realities of new Western wars. But it is another straw in the wind blowing away from war.[8] There is all the more reason for readers to help it gain speed in the coming years.

Notes

Chapter 1 The New Western Way of War from Vietnam to Iraq

1 Theorized in the classic modern work Carl von Clausewitz's *On War*. However, modern warfare in general developed in the later nineteenth and twentieth centuries into industrialized total warfare, harnessing not just the technology but also the social organization of industrial society to produce total mobilization and through it total destruction: see my *Dialectics of War*.

2 Linda R. Robertson, *The Dream of Civilized Warfare: World War I Flying Aces and the American Imagination*.

3 David Edgerton, 'Liberal Militarism and the British State'.

4 Yet totalitarian and authoritarian regimes took the identification of civilians as enemies further: they often saw certain social groups as enemies *as such*, or *in themselves*, to be destroyed for their own sake, rather than for the purposes of militarily defeating a state. The victorious Allies emphasized the difference between their warfare and this practice in the way they prosecuted the defeated powers and (through the UN) codified 'genocide'. However, the degenerate tendency in Western warfare had opened the door to the latter: see my *War and Genocide*, chapter 2.

5 Michael Howard, *Clausewitz*, p. 292. 'Absolute war' was the tendency of war, identified by Clausewitz (*On War*), towards total destruction of the enemy; however, Clausewitz believed it to be limited by the 'friction' in real war.

6 See my discussion in *Dialectics of War*, p. 17.

7 'Western' in a contemporary political sense therefore means belonging to the power bloc or conglomerate centered on the USA, rather than a Western culture. The Western core includes North America, Western Europe, Japan and Australasia; many

other states in East-Central Europe, Latin America, Africa and Asia are more or less integrated. For further discussion, see Martin Shaw, *Theory of the Global State*.

8   Jacques van Doorn, *The Soldier and Social Change*.

9   See my discussion in *Post-Military Society*, chapters 4 and 5. Conscription finally ended in all major Western European countries (except Germany) in the 1990s.

10 Shaw, *Post-Military Society*.

11 This is the most appropriate name (which does not prejudge claims to the islands), adopted by Virginia Gamba, *The Falklands-Malvinas War*. However, when discussing the British campaign, I shall refer to the 'Falklands War', as it is known in Britain.

12 For general accounts, see Lawrence Freedman, *Britain and the Falklands War*, and David Monaghan, *The Falklands War: Myth and Countermyth*.

13 Mary Kaldor, *The Baroque Arsenal*.

14 Imperial War Museum, <http://www.iwm.org.uk/collections/books/bookfaqs14.htm> [6 February 2004].

15 Michael Mandelbaum, 'Vietnam: The Television War'; Daniel Hallin, *The 'Uncensored War': The Media and Vietnam*.

16 David Morrison and Howard Tumber, *Journalists at War: The Dynamics of News Reporting during the Falklands Conflict*.

17 Glasgow University Media Group, *War and Peace News*, p. 143.

18 Lawrence Freedman, cited by Martin Shaw, *Civil Society and Media in Global Crises: Representing Distant Violence*, p. 73.

19 See Melvin Small and J. David Singer, *Resort to Arms: International and Civil Wars 1816–1980*.

20 In the 1980s, the principal US campaigns were relatively small operations in its traditional sphere of influence: the invasions of the small Caribbean island state of Grenada and of Panama to overthrow the government of General Noriega.

21 Here too there are problems of nomenclature. For some, the Iran–Iraq War (1980–88) was the 'First Gulf War' and the war between the USA-led coalition and Iraq (1991) the 'Second Gulf War'; the 2003 war would be the 'Third Gulf War'. However, the 1991 war is widely known as 'the Gulf War' or, in the USA, the 'Persian Gulf War'. It was in fact only the first war of that year: war continued with the Shi'ite and Kurdish insurrections and their repression. So we might better refer, as I argued in my study of the wars (*Civil Society and Media in Global Crises*, chapter 2), to the Iraq wars of 1991. Here, however, I shall conventionally describe the war between the US-led coalition and Iraq as the 'Gulf War'.

22   This is not to suggest that Bush Senior was justified in the policies he adopted. Precisely because there were spontaneous insurrections, the situation was very different. If the USA had protected the insurrections by halting Saddam's force movements and grounding his helicopters, it might have facilitated his overthrow without the need for occupation. The insurrection would have given a new government far more legitimacy than that possessed by the USA and Iraqi authorities in 2003–4.

23   K. Rizer, 'Bombing Dual-Use Targets: Legal, Ethical, and Doctrinal Perspectives'.

24   Shaw, *Civil Society and Media*, part III, *passim*.

25   See Philip Taylor, *War and the Media: Propaganda and Persuasion in the Gulf War*.

26   Cited in Shaw, *Civil Society and Media*, p. 89.

27   See ibid., p. 36.

28   David Rieff, *Slaughterhouse: Bosnia and the Failure of the West*.

29   Nicholas J. Wheeler, *Saving Strangers*.

30   See Linda Melvern, *A People Betrayed: The Role of the West in Rwanda's Genocide*; Michael Barnett, *Eyewitness to a Genocide*.

31   See Jan Willem Honig and Norbert Both, *Srebrenica: Record of a War Crime*.

32   Howard Clark, *Civil Resistance in Kosovo*.

33   International Independent Commission on Kosovo, *The Kosovo Report*.

34   Quoted by Eliot A. Cohen, 'Kosovo and the New American Way of War', p. 60.

35   Quoted by Michael Ignatieff, *Virtual War: Kosovo and Beyond*, p. 3; see also James Der Derian's interview with Clark in *Virtuous War*, pp. 188–98.

36   Thus the term 'Kosovo War' should be used to refer to the whole of this conflict, not just the phase after the NATO intervention.

37   After three months of NATO bombing Milosevic decided to withdraw Serbian forces from Kosovo, leading to the imposition of a UN-run, NATO-policed protectorate in which the Albanian majority dominated political life. The small Serb minority, many of whom had linked their fortunes to Serbian rule, was attacked by Albanians and many were forced to leave.

38   Democratic Republic of Congo (formerly Zaire).

39   184 people are reported killed at the Pentagon. The final New York toll stands at 2,749, and the official list of those missing now matches the number of death certificates issued (*New York Times*, 14 February 2004). The number of missing-person reports had

peaked at 6,886 two weeks after the attack, amid confusion and calls from frantic relatives. The large discrepancy revealed by two years' meticulous record keeping should encourage caution and scepticism in evaluating other casualty estimates.

40 Stephen Biddle, *Afghanistan and the Future of Warfare*. Afghanistan had been at war continuously since 1979, when the USSR invaded the country to support the pro-Soviet government against insurgents, who resisted the occupation with support from Pakistan and the USA. After Soviet forces left in 1989, new civil wars broke out between various mujaheddin warlords and factions, until the Taliban, or 'Students of Islamic Knowledge Movement', gained general dominance in 1996. They never achieved complete territorial control, however, their rule being contested by the Northern Alliance forces that allied with the USA in 2001.

41 Polly Toynbee, *The Guardian*, 31 October, 2001.

42 Unlike Argentina, Iraq and Serbia, Taliban-ruled Afghanistan had few of the characteristics of a modern state, although it claimed the same sovereignty. A backward war-devastated country, its economy was wrecked and its central administration weak. Taliban forces were largely irregular and poorly armed even if al-Qaeda fighters were considerably better trained and more determined.

43 C. Conetta, *Operation Enduring Freedom*.

44 Aldo Benini and Lawrence H. Moulton, 'The Distribution of Civilian Victims'.

45 M. O'Hanlon, 'A Flawed Masterpiece', cited by Mary Kaldor, 'American Power: From "Compellance" to Cosmopolitanism?', p. 7.

46 However, Biddle, *Afghanistan*, plausibly demolishes the claims for a distinctive 'Afghan model' based on the peculiarities of this campaign.

47 Kaldor, 'American Power', p. 7.

Chapter 2 Theories of the New Western Way of War

1 Victor Davis Hanson, *The Western Way of War: Infantry Battle in Classical Greece*, p. 9.

2 Ibid., p. 13.

3 Ibid., pp. 14–15.

4 Ibid., p. 17.

5 Ibid.

6 Ibid., p. 11; emphasis in original.

7 Ibid., p. 228.
8 Ibid., p. 227.
9 Ibid., p. 17.
10 Ibid., p. 10.
11 Hanson has since dropped the critical conclusions in his work that he drew about American warfare in the 1980s. Since 9/11 he has gained attention as a staunch supporter of the Bush administration's new wars, in essays collected as *An Autumn of War: What America Learned from September 11 and the War on Terrorism*, and *Between War and Peace: Lessons from Afghanistan to Iraq*.
12 E. H. Arnett, 'Welcome to Hyperwar'; J. Arquilla and D. Ronfeldt, 'Cyberwar is Coming!'.
13 Thomas Keaney and Eliot A. Cohen, *Gulf War Air Power Survey: A Summary*, p. 238, quoted by Andrew Latham, 'Reimagining Warfare: The "Revolution in Military Affairs"', p. 212.
14 Latham, 'Reimagining Warfare', p. 221.
15 This concept was widely applied. General Wesley K. Clark, former NATO commander in the Kosovo War, saw the lightly armed Palestinian *intifada* as an 'asymmetric war' against Israel's military machine: 'How to Fight an Asymmetric War', *Time*, 23 October 2000. The Global War on Terrorism was recognized as quintessentially asymmetric: thus, as military 'victory' gave way to permanent counter-insurgency in Iraq, Anthony Cordesman noted that it was 'far from clear that the United States can win this kind of asymmetric war': *Iraq and Conflict Termination: The Road to Guerrilla War?*
16 Keaney and Cohen, quoted by Latham, 'Reimagining Warfare', p. 212.
17 Colin S. Gray, *Modern Strategy*.
18 Colin S. Gray, *Strategy for Chaos: Revolutions in Military Affairs and the Evidence of History*.
19 Vincent J. Goulding, Jr., 'Back to the Future with Asymmetric Warfare', p. 21.
20 Lieutenant General Leslie McNair, cited by Cohen, 'Kosovo', p. 40.
21 Ibid., pp. 42–4.
22 Ibid., p. 45.
23 Ibid., p. 51.
24 Ibid., p. 50.
25 Ibid., p. 55.
26 Ibid.
27 Ibid., pp. 55–6.
28 Ibid., p. 59.

29 Eliot A. Cohen, 'World War IV', *Wall Street Journal,* 20 November 2001. Afghanistan was the first campaign of this new world war: the United States should throw its weight behind pro-Western and anti-clerical forces in the Muslim world, beginning with the overthrow of the theocratic state in Iran. For these views Cohen was described as 'the most influential neo-con in academe': <http://rightweb. irc-online.org/ind/cohen/cohen.php> [24 February 2004].

30 'Battlefields' still exist but they are not usually the main spaces in which wars are fought; hence the broader term 'battlespaces': see my *War and Genocide,* chapter 6.

31 J. van Doorn, *The Soldier and Social Change.* Conscripts became superfluous and universal military service was phased out, in Britain in the 1960s, the USA in the 1970s, and most of Western Europe after the end of the Cold War in the 1990s. See my *Post-Military Society.*

32 Charles Moskos and Frank Wood, eds, *The Military: More Than Just a Job?.*

33 Robin Luckham, 'Of Arms and Culture'.

34 Michael Mann, 'The Roots and Contradictions of Modern Militarism'.

35 Shaw, *Post-Military Society.*

36 Mann, 'The Roots', pp. 48–9.

37 Jean Baudrillard, *The Gulf War Did Not Take Place.*

38 Martin Shaw and Roy Carr-Hill, *Public Opinion, Media and Violence: Attitudes to the Gulf War in a Local Population.*

39 E.g., Taylor, *War and the Media.* Some work has descended into crude anti-Western propaganda of its own, e.g., Philip Hammond and Edward S. Herman, eds, *Degraded Capability: The Media and the Kosovo Crisis*; and David Miller, ed., *Tell Me Lies: Propaganda and Media Distortion in the Attack on Iraq.*

40 See my *Civil Society and Media,* chapter 7.

41 Emmanuel Todd, *After the Empire: The Breakdown of the American Order.*

42 Mary Kaldor, *Global Civil Society: An Answer to War.*

43 'At the political level, the alliance held together. At the military level, alliance cohesion was a myth.' Michael Ignatieff, *Virtual War,* p. 207.

44 Ibid., p. 191; emphasis added.

45 Ibid., p. 197.

46 Paul W. Kahn, 'War and Sacrifice in Kosovo', *Philosophy and Public Policy,* 19, spring–summer 1999, quoted in ibid., p. 162.

47 James Der Derian, *Virtuous War,* pp. xiv–xv; emphases in original.

48   Ibid., p. 120.
49   Ibid., pp. xvi–xvii.
50   Ibid., p. 147.
51   Ibid., p. 217.
52   Ibid., p. 219.
53   Ibid., p. 221.
54   Martin Shaw, *Dialectics of War*, n. 3. The reference is to Marx's first *Thesis on Feuerbach*.
55   See my *Dialectics of War*, chapter 1.
56   Michael Howard (in *Clausewitz*) showed how his argument that war tended towards the absolute could be used to pinpoint the dilemmas of nuclear war. In turn I used Howard's reading of the nuclear dilemma, that 'all traditional constraints on "absolute war" have been removed and its complete realisation has for the first time become a practical possibility', to argue that, 'In reaching this limit, war also negates itself. If there are no longer internal constraints, and war becomes absolute destruction, it becomes invalid as a means of policy. . . . [Hence m]uch of modern strategy can be seen as an attempt to avoid redundancy . . . envisaging limited wars short of total nuclear war.' *Dialectics of War*, p. 17.
57   Mary Kaldor, 'Warfare and Capitalism'.
58   Ibid., p. 283.
59   Ibid., pp. 284–5.
60   Anthony Giddens, *The Nation-State and Violence*. The other clusters centred on capitalism, industrialism and surveillance.
61   Michael Mann, *The Sources of Social Power*, vol. 1. The other sources were economic, political and ideological.
62   This follows the framework I developed in *Dialectics of War*, supplemented by the typology of war in *War and Genocide*.
63   Clearly the understanding of warfare, economy, polity, ideology and culture, for example, as distinct arenas of social life is a way of making sense of complex realities, both for actors and for theorists. In reality, actors, areas of action and social institutions 'belong' to more than one domain. For example, arms manufacturers, workers, firms and their production can be seen as part of the 'mode of warfare', but they also belong to the 'mode of production', and they participate in the political and cultural spheres. Insofar as arms production is inherently connected to war preparation, we will fail to understand its significance if we treat it exclusively or mainly as 'economic' activity. However, we will also treat its significance too narrowly if we fail to grasp its embeddedness in economy, polity and culture.

64 For example, Peter Calvocoressi and Guy Wint, *Total War: Causes and Courses of the Second World War*; I. F. W. Beckett, 'Total War', in Colin McInnes and G. D. Sheffield, eds, *Warfare in the Twentieth Century: Theory and Practice*; Arthur Marwick, ed., *Total War and Social Change*.

65 'In the present Convention, genocide means any of the following acts committed with intent to destroy, in whole or in part, a national, ethnical, racial or religious group, as such': United Nations, *Convention*, Article II.

Chapter 3   The Global Surveillance Mode of Warfare

1   For example, International Institute of Strategic Studies, *The Military Balance*, published annually; Dan Smith with Ane Bræin, *The Atlas of War and Peace*.

2   Mary Kaldor and Asbjorn Eide, eds, *The World Military Order: The Impact of Military Technology on the Third World*.

3   David Held et al., *Global Transformations*, p. 88.

4   Ibid., p. 89.

5   Ibid.

6   Ibid., pp. 101–3.

7   Ibid., pp. 121–3.

8   Ibid., pp. 124–6.

9   See the map in Martin Shaw, *Theory of the Global State*, p. 204.

10 Indeed many national nuclear capabilities have been developed and maintained more for the status they give than for their potential uses in war: for political rather than military reasons.

11 Gilbert Achcar, in 'The Strategic Triad: The United States, Russia and China', argued that, in US military planning for twin wars, Iraq and North Korea were substitutes for the 'real' enemies, Russia and China. After the Bush administration's difficulties in managing the 2003 Iraq War and its aftermath simultaneously with the North Korean missile crisis, this idea is less plausible.

12 For critiques, see Tarak Barkawi and Mark Laffey, eds, *Democracy, Liberalism and War: Rethinking the Democratic Peace Debate*.

13 Mark Duffield, *Global Governance and the New Wars*.

14 Mary Kaldor, *New and Old Wars: Organized Violence in a Global Era*.

15 'Globalization' is, of course, a contested concept. However, although the exaggerated claims of 'hyperglobalizers' about the demise of the nation-state have been much criticized, there is a

considerable degree of consensus that there is a 'global transformation' of state power as well as economy and society. See Held et al., *Global Transformations*: pp. 1–28. But the general globalization literature has lamentably marginalized warfare: Held et al., *Global Transformations*, is virtually the only 'globalization' study to discuss its military dimensions. My own *Theory of the Global State* offers an account of 'global transformation' centred on military–political relations.

16 Duffield, *Global Governance*, p. 52; except for academics, his list is taken from Karin Von Hippel, *Democracy by Force*.

17 Kaldor, *Old and New Wars*, chapter 1. However, she went some way to acknowledging that modern war was *more* than Clausewitzian: 'Clausewitz could not possibly have envisaged the awesome combination of mass production, mass politics and mass communications when harnessed to mass production.' For a fuller critique, see my 'The Contemporary Mode of Warfare? Mary Kaldor's Theory of New Wars'.

18 For example, Kaldor sees Clausewitz's emphasis on battle as outdated. In my view, while battle's *meaning* has changed (aerial bombing delivers a rather different kind of decisive encounter from horses and artillery), and global political, legal and media surveillance imposes new *constraints*, battle remains important. Kaldor's example is the Bosnian war: but in my view the battles of 1995 in which the Croatian and Bosnian armies forced back the Serbians were of considerable importance to the outcome of the war.

19 Andrew Latham, 'Reimagining Warfare: the "Revolution in Military Affairs"', pp. 221–3, which draws on my *Dialectics of War*. Clearly Latham was writing before 9/11 and the amalgamation of the 'rogue' threat into global 'terrorism'.

20 Ibid., p. 223.

21 'Totalitarianism' – the most extreme kind of militarized politics – expressed this 'total' war relationship to the fullest extent.

22 Hence the core plausibility of Edward Thompson's thesis of 'exterminism' ('Exterminism, the Last Stage of Civilization'), even if in other respects it was inadequate: see Shaw, 'From Total War to Democratic Peace: Exterminism and Historical Pacifism', in H. Kaye and K. McClelland, eds, *E. P. Thompson: Critical Debates*, pp. 233–51.

23 Hence the idea of the 'competition state' developed in international political economy: for a critical discussion, see my *Theory of the Global State*, chapter 3.

24 In *The Nation-State and Violence*, Giddens saw surveillance as occurring primarily within the national state context, even if he

saw the potential for its wider expansion. Today, surveillance is increasingly global, occurring simultaneously through national, international and transnational institutions and mechanisms.

25   'Global' includes *all* of these 'levels': it is not identical with 'world-wide' or (as Held et al., *Global Transformations*, incorrectly suggest) 'intercontinental' types of relations. See my *Theory of the Global State*, chapter 1, for elaboration.

26   These ideal-typical 'ways of warfare' correspond, except for the 'terrorist', to the types of state identified in *Theory of the Global State*, chapter 7: the Western-global state; quasi-imperial nation-states; and new states.

27   For a survey of these trends, see Held et al., *Global Transformations*, pp. 115–23.

28   Wars between established states are by no means impossible, but their international costs have been considerably raised. No lengthy struggle like the 1980–88 Iraq–Iran War has been fought since the end of the Cold War.

29   So, for example, British 'area bombing' of German cities was designed to destroy civilian morale by creating fear. Israeli attacks on targets in Palestinian residential areas are designed to intimidate the civilian population as well as to kill enemy combatants.

30   Brigitte L. Nacos, *Mass-Mediated Terrorism: The Central Role of the Media in Terrorism and Counter-Terrorism*, especially chapter 3.

31   Hence, for example, once audiences were habituated to suicide killings by young men, in 2003 a Palestinian group produced the first *female* suicide bomber, to maintain the shock element. They followed her with a *young mother* suicide bomber.

32   To gauge this leap, consider that the almost 3,000 killed by al-Qaeda in New York and Washington roughly equalled the total death toll in thirty years of killing by all sides in the Northern Ireland terrorist war. As Christopher Hitchens wrote, the 9/11 killers could have hoped to kill many more, up to 100,000, or 'a Dresden for the Taliban' ('Murder Was their only Motive', *The Guardian*, October 2001).

33   This view of ethnic cleansing as genocide has been asserted legally in decisions of the International Criminal Tribunal for Further Yugoslavia (see William Schabas, *Genocide in International Law*, pp. 197–8), although it remains controversial (as indicated by Schabas's following discussion). However, from a sociological point of view this is the only plausible way of understanding 'ethnic cleansing': see the discussion in my forthcoming book *Genocide* (Cambridge: Polity).

34 For these categories, see Stanley Cohen, *States of Denial*, chapter 1.

35 In this table I have further distinguished actors following a 'national-militarist' way of war between nuclear-armed and non-nuclear states, because the nuclear threshold has proved important for defining the probability of war between actors.

36 Technologies do not determine warfare; rather methods are chosen with global surveillance and political effect in mind.

37 A major war between the West and one of the principal non-Western states, e.g., China, is clearly a theoretical possibility but it does not have a name in official Western discourse.

38 The most likely outcome for these campaigns is that their ideological frameworks will mutate, amplifying their ideas and objectives to maintain their political coherences.

Chapter 4   Rules of Risk-Transfer War

1 Of course the Vietnam War was a total war for North Vietnam and the National Liberation Front/Vietcong and for Vietnamese society.

2 In practice this was increasingly acknowledged, although of course ultimately it remains uncertain.

3 Although this did not always work: witness the defeat of Winston Churchill, Britain's wartime prime minister, and his Conservative Party in the 1945 general election.

4 Remember that here I am comparing Western publics with those in non-Western states: all this is relative. Of course it still allows for manipulation, and Western states have more sophisticated ways of achieving this than other states.

5 Of course counter-insurgency *is*, confusingly, still part of the global 'war' on terror. Here there is an assertion, albeit one that confuses the facts of bloody conflict, of the difference between literal, physical warfare and ideological and political 'war'.

6 United Nations High Commission for Refugees, 2002.

7 Refugees are internationally displaced people. 'Internally displaced persons', refugees by another name, remain within their state of origin.

8 Even Western states that still maintain conscription, such as Germany and (until recently) France, do not deploy conscripts in combat situations.

9 J. McKitrick et al., cited by Andrew Latham, 'Reimagining Warfare', p. 225.

10 Certainly the Falklands-Malvinas War showed that the United Kingdom also retains the political, as well as military capacity to fight this kind of war semi-independently, and the same is true of France. Episodes such as the British intervention in Sierra Leone and the French in Ivory Coast have demonstrated, in fairly small ways, a continuing warfighting potential. The UN intervention in Bosnia-Herzegovina (1992–5) was primarily an Anglo-French-Dutch operation.

11 See for example Fabrice Weissman, ed., *In the Shadow of 'Just Wars': Violence, Politics and Humanitarian Action.*

12 See my *Post-Military Society*, chapter 1. Militarism is a concept of social organization, not merely of ideology; thus we can identify 'democratic' as well as authoritarian militarisms.

13 Anthony Giddens, *The Consequences of Modernity.*

14 Quoted in Michael Howard, *Clausewitz*, p. 25.

15 Giddens, *The Consequences of Modernity.*

16 Ulrich Beck, *Risk Society*, p. 28.

17 Ulrich Beck, 'Risk Society Revisited', p. 215.

18 B. Adam, U. Beck and J. van Loon, 'Introduction: Repositioning Risk; the Challenge for Social Theory', p. 1.

19 Ibid., p. 7.

20 Beck, 'Risk Society Revisited', p. 224; emphasis added. Thus, although Beck is known for his statement that 'poverty is hierarchic, smog is democratic' (*Risk Society*, p. 36), he recognizes differences of risk position. The difference between him and his critics seems to be about how far, as Douglas has put it, 'Perceptions of high risk reinforce already existing social divisions' (quoted in Alan Scott, 'Risk Society or Angst Society?'). Clearly, pre-existing social locations – national, ethnic and political even more than class – condition marked inequalities of risk in war. However, risk definition, i.e., how political leaders and military commanders define the need to attack or protect particular groups as *they* identify them, is the crucial process creating differential life-risks.

21 Beck's work contains few pointers to the significance of his theory for war: for an illuminating discussion, see Hans Joas, 'War and the Risk Society', in his *War and Modernity*, pp. 171–9.

22 Beck, 'Risk Society Revisited', p. 215.

Chapter 5 Iraq: Risk Economy of a War

1 This was a misnomer. Pre-emptive war is generally understood as action to stall an imminent threat. What Bush was proposing was preventative war, to prevent a threat from emerging.

2   The growing international opposition to sanctions had led the USA and the UK in 2001–2 to propose 'smart sanctions', intended to target the regime but spare the people.

3   Middle East Watch, *Genocide in Iraq: The Anfal Campaign Against the Kurds*. States have a duty to 'prevent and punish' genocide; however, Saddam's acts were committed in the 1980s and early 1990s, and punishing the perpetrators implied legal not military action.

4   Quoted by John Kampfner, *Blair's Wars*, p. 155.

5   Quoted in ibid., p. 156.

6   A case for action on grounds of human rights was never made by the USA or the UK, or indeed by states such as France and Germany that rejected the WMD case. Of course any human rights case could have found difficulty gaining Russian and Chinese support in the Security Council.

7   The administration made much of the presence of a small Islamist faction, Anwar-al-Islam, allegedly linked to al-Qaeda and fighting Saddam's Kurdish enemies, in territory in north-eastern Iraq (but outside Saddam's control), although this hardly proved a link between al-Qaeda and Saddam. US and Kurdish forces ousted Anwar-al-Islam from the area they controlled in March 2003.

8   Dana Milbank and Claudia Deane, 'Hussein Link to 9/11 Lingers in Many Minds', *Washington Post*, 6 September 2003.

9   Todd Gittlin, 'Globalization, Education and Media: Notes on the Circulation of Media'.

10   Michael Ignatieff, 'Friends Disunited', *The Guardian*, 24 March 2003.

11   Paul Krugman, 'I Do Get Rattled', *The Guardian*, 19 September 2003, citing Henry Kissinger.

12   Jessica Mathews and Joseph Cirincione, 'Q & A on Iraq's Weapons Programs'.

13   Polly Toynbee, 'If the UN Signs up to War, We Will Have to Back it Too', *The Guardian*, 12 February 2003.

14   Oliver Burkeman and Julian Borger, 'War Critics Astounded as US Hawk Admits Invasion was Illegal', *The Guardian*, 20 November 2003.

15   When NATO acted without prior UN authorization over Kosovo, it could claim tacit support because the Security Council decisively rejected a resolution attacking its actions. Over Iraq, the USA and the UK simply could not muster a majority in the council, nor could they claim the existence of a humanitarian emergency, so the manifest illegitimacy of their actions was greater.

16   Shaw, *Theory of the Global State*.

17   Michael Mann, *Incoherent Empire*.

18   I develop this argument in a preface to the Italian translation of *Theory of the Global State*, *La rivoluzione incompiuta: democrazia e stato nell'era della globalità*. Milan: Università Bocconi Editore, 2004.

19   Mann, *Incoherent Empire*, p. 200.

20   Robert Dreyfuss, 'Just the Beginning: Is Iraq the Opening Salvo in a War to Remake the World?' *American Prospect*, 1 April 2003.

21   Charlotte Denny, 'Greenspan Blames Threat of War for Recovery Delay', *The Guardian*, 12 February 2003.

22   Larry Elliott, 'Bank Begins to Compile War's Casualty List', *The Guardian*, 13 February 2003.

23   The fast growth in the US and UK economies later in the year (in the third quarter of 2003, the US economy grew at 7.2 per cent per annum) may have reflected a 'bounce' back from the nervousness of the war period.

24   Archbishops of Canterbury and Westminster, joint statement, 20 February 2003.

25   Leaked reports of these UN estimates were posted on the website of the UK-based anti-war group Campaign against Sanctions in Iraq; UN o.fficials did not challenge their authenticity. Jonathan Steele, 'Counting the Dead', *The Guardian*, 29 January 2003.

26   Medact, quoted in ibid.

27   Amnesty poster [seen 14 March 2003].

28   The best estimate of its size was a survey-based calculation of 1.4 million: D. Gordon, 'Iraq, War and Morality'.

29   Tony Blair, 'I Want to Solve the Iraq Issue via the United Nations', 15 February 2003, <http://www.labour.org.uk/tbglasgow> [17 November 2003].

30   Yousif Al-Khoei, 'The Shia Factor', *Iraq Crisis Report*, 1; <http://www.iwpr.net> [17 November 2003].

31   Only occasionally did someone stand apart from this logic to argue 'that it is wrong to engage in the . . . killing of a few innocent people in order to save the many.' Gordon, 'Iraq, War and Morality'.

32   For anti-war leaders, too, the risk economy was also partly about maximizing electoral advantage. Chancellor Gerhard Schröder secured somewhat unexpected re-election in late 2002 by proclaiming that Germany would not be involved in an Iraq War. President Jacques Chirac of France consolidated his domestic popularity by putting himself in the forefront of international opposition. President Vladimir Putin of Russia avoided any clash with Russian public opinion by joining with France and Germany.

33   Kampfner, *Blair's Wars*, pp. 152, 168.

34   Andrew Rawnsley, 'And Now for the Home Front', *The Observer*, 20 April 2003.

35   'Contingency plans were prepared – to which Donald Rumsfeld clumsily alluded – for scrubbing a British contribution to the war.' Ibid.

36   Patrick Wintour, 'Short Spearheads Rebellion with Threat to Quit over War', *The Guardian*, 10 March 2003. Despite this outburst Blair felt unable to sack Short; indeed he persuaded her to stay in the government until the end of the war. Only later did she finally resign, having been perhaps somewhat reckless with her own political credibility.

37   Mary Kaldor, 'American Power: From "Compellance" to Cosmopolitanism?', p. 7.

38   'Britain Will Pay "Blood Price" – Blair', 9 September 2002, <http://news.bbc.co.uk/1/hi/uk_politics/2239887.stm>   [11 February 2003].

39   Williamson Murray and Robert H. Scales, *The Iraq War: A Military History*, pp. 92–3.

40   Harlan Ullman, 'Shock Tactics', *The Guardian*, 25 March 2003 [interview].

41   Murray and Scales, *The Iraq War*, p. 196.

42   Iraq Coalition Casualty Count, <http://lunaville.org/warcasualties/Summary.aspx> [21 November 2003].

43   Carl Conetta, *The Wages of War: Iraqi Combatant and Noncombatant Fatalities in the 2003 Conflict*; emphasis added.

44   Hugo Slim, 'Why Protect Civilians? Innocence, Immunity and Enmity in War', p. 501.

45   Associated Press, 'In the Kuwaiti Desert' [International Justice Watch Discussion List, 4 February 2003].

46   'The Baghdad Blogger', *The Guardian*, 26 March 2003.

47   Julian Borger and Stuart Millar, 'It Sounds Surgical in Theory', *The Guardian*, 9 April 2003.

48   Conetta, *The Wages of War*.

49   Associated Press, 'In the Kuwaiti Desert'.

50   See, for example, William Branigin, 'A Gruesome Scene on Highway 9: 10 Dead After Vehicle Shelled at Checkpoint', *Washington Post*, 1 April 2003.

51   Robert Fisk, 'US Troops Turn Botched Saddam Raid into a Massacre', *The Independent*, 28 July 2003.

52   Jeff Wilkinson, 'Destruction of Iraqi Homes within "Rules of War," Spokesman Says', *Dallas-Fort Worth Star-Telegram*, 19 November 2003.

53 US forces acknowledged the extent of harm by a system of pay-
    ments from commanders' discretionary funds: by November 2003,
    $1,540,050 had been handed over for personal injury, death or
    damage to property, in payouts averaging a few hundred dollars.
    According to the military, 'Payments will only be made for non-
    combat related activities and instances where soldiers have acted
    negligently or wrongfully.' Rory McCarthy, 'US Pays up for Fatal
    Iraq Blunders', *The Guardian*, 26 November 2003.
54 *Today*, BBC Radio 4, 3 April 2003.
55 Richard Norton-Taylor and Owen Bowcott, 'British Use of Cluster
    Bombs Condemned', *The Guardian*, 3 April 2003.
56 Human Rights Watch, *Off Target: The Conduct of the War and
    Civilian Casualties in Iraq*.
57 Jason Vest, 'U.S. Army Documents Warn of Occupation Hazards:
    The War After the War', *Village Voice*, 19–25 March 2003.
58 Douglas C. Lovelace (director, Strategic Services Institute),
    'Forword', to C. C. Crane and A. W. Terrill, *Reconstructing Iraq:
    Insights, Challenges, and Missions for Military Forces in a Post-
    Conflict Scenario*, p. iv.
59 Crane and Terrill, *Reconstructing Iraq*, p. 42.
60 Marina Ottaway, 'A Real Plan for Rebuilding Iraq', *International
    Herald Tribune*, 3 March 2003.
61 Robert Fisk, 'Losing the Peace', *The Independent*, 31 July 2003. Of
    course, lawlessness was probably not helped by the emptying of
    the prisons in Saddam's final days.
62 An extraordinary feature was the death toll from celebratory
    gunfire: it was claimed that in Baghdad, 'from July through
    September alone, 2,175 locals died.' Awadh al-Tae'e, 'Gun
    Culture Under Fire', *Iraq Crisis Report*, 36; <www.iwpr.net> [21
    November 2003].
63 Medact, *Continuing Collateral Damage: The Health and Environ-
    mental Costs of War on Iraq 2003*, p. 14; <http://www.medact.org/
    tbx/pages/sub.cfm?id=775> [17 November 2003].
64 Ibid.
65 Department for International Development (DfID), Iraq Update,
    24 April 2003; <http://www.dfid.gov.uk/News/PressReleases/files/
    iraq_update> [10 September 2003].
66 Ibid.
67 Medact, *Continuing Collateral Damage*, p. 8.
68 Mann, *Incoherent Empire*, p. 184.
69 It is emblazoned over the home page of <www.iraqbodycount.
    net>.

70   Gen. Franks, statement at Bagram airbase, *San Francisco Chronicle*, 23 March 2002; <http://www.globalsecurity.org/org/news/2002/020323-attack01.htm> [26 January 2004].

71   United States Department of Defense, 'Fallen Warriors', <http://www.defendamerica.gov/fallen.html> [21 March 2004].

72   Ministry of Defence, 'Details of British Casualties', <http://www.operations.mod.uk/telic/casualties.htm>   [21 November 2003].

73   For example, Iraq Coalition Casualty Count and CNN sites, already cited.

74   Iraq Body Count, 'Rationale', <http://www.iraqbodycount.net/background.htm rationale> [23 March 2004].

75   The logic here is sound insofar as the life of each individual affected is of equal value; but wounds can vary greatly in their severity and their implications for the person's life.

76   In these wars, the claim is true only in a wider sense, namely that larger numbers of civilians are affected by the displacement, hardship and illness caused by war-disruption.

77   Emphases added.

78   Conetta, *Wages of War*. He does not explore why a 'casualty toll' should be of greater 'strategic significance for policy' than other sorts of information.

79   Gunther Grass, *Crabwalk*, p. 162.

80   Julian Barnes, 'This War Was Not Worth a Child's Finger', *The Guardian*, 11 April 2003.

81   Iraq Body Count reported fifteen different projects at varying stages of completion in mid-2003; 'Counting the Human Cost', <http://www.iraqbodycount.net/editorial_june1203.htm>   [23 March 2004].

82   Aldo Benini and L. H. Moulton, 'The Distribution of Civilian Victims in an Asymmetrical Conflict: Operation Enduring Freedom, Afghanistan'.

83   IBC comment ('Counting the Cost'): 'Due to real-world limitations of time, money and human resources, there is an inherent conflict between these two approaches. The more direct a project is and the fuller and higher quality its evidence, the less practical it is for it also to be exhaustive and complete; and the more comprehensive a study aims to be, the less likely that it can also be as detailed and as fine-grained in the evidence it collects as a "direct" project. This makes it pointless to ask which is "better". Different types of project are needed. . . . Putting all the projects together can strengthen their total impact.'

84 A maximum of 7,356 were deaths in the invasion phase up
    to and including 1 May 2003: <http://www.iraqbodycount.net/
    editorial_feb0704.htm> [17 March 2004].
85 They noted that '8,000 of [the] injuries were in the Baghdad area
    alone, suggesting that the full, countrywide picture, as with deaths,
    is yet to emerge.' However, since the 'highly-targeted bombing of
    Baghdad in the early days of the conflict may have injured far more
    people than were killed', it could also be that injury tolls else-
    where, or in later periods, might not be proportional.
86 <http://www.iraqbodycount.net/editorial_feb0704.htm>   [17
    March 2004].
87 Conetta, *Wages of War*. It is noteworthy that IBC founder John
    Sloboda has subsequently commended Conetta's study, as attempt-
    ing 'to provide a total fatality estimate corrected for problems of bias
    and incompleteness. By contrast, Iraq Body Count provides a com-
    prehensive survey of incidents and estimates as reported in various
    media.' (Email to <naspir@yahoogroups.com>, 18 February 2004.)
88 Here his estimate comprised three data reviews, drawing on field
    observations and casualty estimates by US military personnel and
    embedded reporters; assessing the impact of aerial bombardment;
    and assessing the likely fatal effects of coalition long-range artillery,
    drawing on operational data and metrics for artillery effectiveness.
    'No one of these data reviews provides a complete picture',
    Conetta argues. 'Their fusion, however, serves as a basis for extrap-
    olating total Iraqi combatant fatalities' (*Wages of War*).
89 In particular, he emphasizes that, 'in assessing and "adjusting" the
    estimates offered by field observers we have sought to control for
    casualty inflation – a prevalent form of bias.' This seems prudent,
    since we know from many other cases that early reports often over-
    state tolls: the '7,000' victims initially estimated after 9/11 shrank
    to just 3,000 when fuller information was available.
90 Conetta models the non-combatant population of the city into
    four different 'risk groups' of unequal size:

    • those at risk anywhere due to strategic bombardment – a very
      large group;
    • those additionally at risk because they lived in the path of the
      two major American advances into the city – a sizable group;
    • those at high risk because they sought to flee the city in vehi-
      cles during the American advance;
    • those at high risk because they moved openly in the city during
      the final American assaults.

'Only the last group', Conetta argues, 'would have been predominantly male.'

91   Conetta, *Wages of War*.

92   John Mueller, quoted by Edward Helmore, 'Bombers Could Cost Bush the White House', *The Observer*, 24 August 2003.

93   The attempts of the 'body counters' to add up the casualties among Iraqi non-combatants had probably produced only small effects on public opinion. The novelty of 'real time' research and constant updating of statistics had certainly contributed to awareness of life-risks, but mainly among relatively educated minorities who searched the Internet and read serious newspapers. They may have strengthened activist groups who opposed the war, but there is scant evidence for a large contribution to the risk rebound that the US administration was suffering.

94   Indeed these accounted for most deaths of British soldiers from all causes up to November 2003: out of a total of fifty-two, twenty-six were due to these causes compared to only nineteen from hostile action (Ministry of Defence, 'Details of British Casualties').

95   Mann, *Incoherent Empire*, pp. 24–5.

96   <http://edition.cnn.com/SPECIALS/2003/iraq/forces/casualties/index.html> [17 March 2004].

97   Andrew Stephen, 'Paul Bremer Has a New Mission', *New Statesman*, 24 November 2003.

98   Andrew Stephen, 'The US Military Now Puts Machine-Guns into the Hands of Mercenaries', *New Statesman*, 26 April 2004.

99   The murder of four private security operatives triggered the US assault on Fallujah in April 2004.

100   *The Guardian*, 17 March 2004.

101   There was no reason to suppose that they had: al-Qaeda had historically been strongly opposed to Saddam's more secular nationalist regime.

102   Dan Plesch and Richard Norton-Taylor, 'Straw, Powell Had Serious Doubts over their Iraqi Weapons Claims', *The Guardian*, 31 May 2003.

103   *Iraq's Weapons of Mass Destruction – The Assessment of the British Government*, <http://www.number-10.gov.uk/output/Page271.asp> [17 November 2003].

104   Ironically, Dr Kelly, a former UNSCOM weapons inspector, was himself said 'to have been confident evidence of Iraq's banned weapons programme would be found' (Richard Norton-Taylor, 'Outing of Scientist Approved "at the Top"', *The Guardian*, 22 July 2003).

105   Hutton Inquiry (Investigation into the Circumstances Surround-
      ing the Death of Dr David Kelly), <http://www.the-hutton-
      inquiry.org.uk> [17 November 2003].
106   Speech in Cincinnati, 7 October 2002, quoted by Mathews and
      Cirincione, 'Q & A'.
107   Blair was then obliged to set up a similar inquiry into British intel-
      ligence on WMDs.
108   *Comprehensive Report of the Special Advisor to the DCI on Iraq's
      WMD*, <http://www.cia.gov/cia/reports/iraq-wmd-2004>.
109   In 2002, an Indonesian Islamist group linked to al-Qaeda had
      destroyed a nightclub in Bali, killing over 200 mainly Australian
      tourists. However, this was before the Iraq war and there was no
      particular link to Iraq.
110   Although the opposition socialists had been closing on the gov-
      ernment in final opinion polls, commentators attributed their sur-
      prise victory to increased turn-out, stimulated by the attacks,
      and above all to the government's clumsy attempts to blame the
      Basque separatist group, ETA. The crisis reminded Spanish voters
      of their earlier opposition to the government over the war.
111   Richard Clarke, *Against All Enemies*.
112   Julian Borger, 'Interview: Richard Clarke', *The Guardian*, 23
      March 2004.

Chapter 6   A Way of War in Crisis

1   As the US Department of Defense 'Defend America: Fallen
    Heroes' website put it, in a bizarre but revealing reversal, 'Sept.
    11, 2001, marked the beginning of the war against terrorism. But
    it also brought to a tragic end a multitude of lives';
    <http://www.defendamerica.gov/fallen.html> [21 November
    2003]. By 15 March 2004, this statement no longer appeared on
    the site, which had been renamed 'Fallen Warriors'.
2   The end of the Cold War had challenged Western leaders to
    develop new stories about world order. Traditional ideas were first
    repackaged in the loose rhetoric of the 'new world order', but this
    gave no strong direction for future war. Later, ideas of 'humani-
    tarian intervention' provided a stronger ideological framework.
    Few saw humanitarianism as involving repeated wars, and it was
    hardly a compelling ideology for many in US and Western politi-
    cal and military elites.
3   Statement by the military spokesman for al-Qaeda in Europe,
    Abu Dujan al Afghani, Associated Press, 14 March 2004,

<http://www.nytimes.com/2004/03/14/international/europe/14 WIRE-QATAPE.html?ex=1081483200&en=e4cd73006599 e6dc&ei=5070> [7 April 2004].

4 Ibid.

5 See table 3.3 above. Of course al-Qaeda statements also involve denial, for example of the innocence of most of their individual victims, but it is of a different order from the more common, especially Western, minimization of violence itself.

6 Richard Falk, 'In Defense of "Just War" Thinking', *The Nation*, 24 December 2001.

7 Michael Walzer, *Just and Unjust Wars*, p. 136.

8 Hanson, *The Western Way of War*, pp. 14–15.

9 Walzer, *Just and Unjust Wars*, p. 136. True, Walzer is prepared to countenance the extension of combatant status to civilian munitions workers in their workplaces, while they are actually making weapons, and he is also prepared to say that this 'plausible line . . . may be too finely drawn' (p. 146); emphasis in original.

10 Ibid., p. 153.

11 Ibid.

12 Ibid., pp. 153–4.

13 Some forms, at least, of action on the ground, especially on the lines of armed policing, offer the opportunity to discriminate more and avoid civilian casualties to a greater extent. However, here too armed soldiers have an inherent advantage over civilians: as we have seen, this has led to self-protective, 'shoot first, ask questions later', killing of civilians suspected of being insurgents.

14 Notoriously in Rwanda in 1994 and at Srebrenica, Bosnia, in 1995.

15 Walzer, *Just and Unjust Wars*, p. 154.

16 For further discussion, see my *War and Genocide*, chapter 1.

17 There is certainly some evidence to suggest this. The enhanced concern to protect Western soldiers' lives is in itself a historic change: it reflects the outcry over the deaths of GIs in Vietnam, and a rejection of the idea of 'cannon fodder' in favour of the notion of soldiers' rights.

18 International Criminal Tribunal for Former Yugoslavia, *Final Report to the Prosecutor by the Committee Established to Review the NATO Bombing Campaign Against the Federal Republic of Yugoslavia*, <http://www.un.org/icty/pressreal/nato061300.htm> [17 January 2002].

19 See my *Dialectics of War*, chapter 5.

Postscript

1 Edison-Mitofsky survey, *International Herald-Tribune*, 5 November 2004.
2 US presidents cannot seek a third term.
3 Les Roberts, Riyadh Lafta, Richard Garfield, Jamal Khudhairi and Gilbert Burnham, 'Mortality Before and After the 2003 Invasion of Iraq: Cluster Sample Survey', *The Lancet*, 364, pubd online 29 October 2004, <http://image.thelancet.com/extras/04art10342web.pdf> [15 November 2004].
4 The authors acknowledged the study's possible limitations: 'Most importantly, the quality of the data about births, deaths and household composition is dependent on the accuracy of the interviews' (ibid., p. 6).
5 Sheila M. Bird, 'Military and Public-Health Sciences Need to Ally', *The Lancet*, 364. <http://www.thelancet.com/journal/vol364/iss9448/full/llan.364.9448.analysis_and_interpretation.31310.1> [29 November 2004].
6 Roberts et al., 'Mortality', p. 8.
7 <http://www.countthecasualties.org.uk> [8 December 2004].
8 However, this is a useful initiative and, despite my reservations about body counting, I was a founder signatory of the campaign's appeal.

References and Bibliography

Achcar, G. (1998) 'The Strategic Triad: The United States, Russia and China', *New Left Review*, 228, pp. 91–127.

Adam, B., U. Beck and J. van Loon (2000), 'Introduction: Repositioning Risk; the Challenge for Social Theory', in Adam, Beck and van Loon, eds, *Risk Society and Beyond*. London: Sage, pp. 1–32.

Ali, T. (2003) *Bush in Babylon: The Recolonisation of Iraq.* London: Verso.

Arnett, E. H. (1992) 'Welcome to Hyperwar', *Bulletin of the Atomic Scientists*, 48, 7, 1992, pp. 14–21.

Arquilla, J., and D. Ronfeldt (1993) 'Cyberwar is Coming!', *Comparative Strategy*, 12, 2.

Barkawi, T., and M. Laffey, eds (2001) *Democracy, Liberalism and War: Rethinking the Democratic Peace Debate.* Boulder, CO: Lynne Rienner.

Barnett, M. (2003) *Eyewitness to a Genocide.* London: Cornell University Press.

Baudrillard, J. (1995) *The Gulf War Did Not Take Place.* Sydney: Power Publishers.

Beck, U. (1992) *Risk Society.* London: Sage.

—— (2000) 'Risk Society Revisited', in B. Adam, U. Beck and J. van Loon, eds, *Risk Society and Beyond*. London: Sage, pp. 211–29.

Benini, A. A., and L. H. Moulton (2004) 'The Distribution of Civilian Victims in an Asymmetrical Conflict: Operation Enduring Freedom, Afghanistan', *Journal of Peace Research*, 41, pp. 403–22.

Biddle, S. (2002) *Afghanistan and the Future of Warfare.* Carlisle, PA: Strategic Services Institute <http://www.carlisle.army.mil/ssi/pdffiles/00106.pdf> [19 August 2004].

Blaikie, P., T. Cannon, I. Davis and B. Wisner (2003) *At Risk: Natural Hazards, People's Vulnerability and Disasters.* London: Routledge.

Calvocoressi, P., and G. Wint (1972) *Total War: Causes and Courses of the Second World War.* London: Allen Lane.

Carnegie Endowment for International Peace (2003) 'From Victory to Success: Afterwar Policy in Iraq', *Foreign Policy*, July–August.

Clark, H. (2000) *Civil Resistance in Kosovo*. London: Pluto.

Clarke, R. (2004) *Against All Enemies: Inside America's War on Terror*, New York: Free Press.

Clausewitz, C. von ([1831] 1976) *On War*, ed. P. Paret and M. Howard. Princeton, NJ: Princeton University Press.

Coates, D., and Krieger, J. (2004) *Blair's War*. Cambridge: Polity.

Cohen, E. A. (2001) 'Kosovo and the New American Way of War', in A. J. Bacevich and E. A. Cohen, *War over Kosovo*. New York: Columbia University Press.

—— (ed.) (2001) *Gulf War Air Power Survey*, vol. I: *Planning and Command and Control*. Washington DC: Government Reprints Press.

Cohen, S. (2000) *States of Denial*. Cambridge: Polity.

Cole, J. (2003) 'The United States and Shi'ite Religious Factions in Post-Ba'athist Iraq', *Middle East Journal*, 57, pp. 543–66.

Conetta, C. (2002) *Operation Enduring Freedom: Why a Higher Rate of Civilian Bombing Casualties*. Cambridge, MA: Project on Defense Alternatives; <http://www.comw.org/pda/0201oef.html>.

—— (2003) *The Wages of War: Iraqi Combatant and Noncombatant Fatalities in the 2003 Conflict*. Cambridge, MA: Project on Defense Alternatives; <http://www.comw.org/pda/0310rm8.html>.

—— (2004) *Disappearing the Dead: Iraq, Afghanistan, and the Idea of a 'New Warfare'*. Cambridge, MA: Project on Defense Alternatives; <http://www.comw.org/pda/0402rm9.html>.

Cook, R. (2003) *Point of Departure*. London: Simon & Schuster.

Cordesman, A. (2003) *The Iraq War: A Working Chronology*. Washington, DC: Center for Strategic and International Studies.

—— (2003) *Iraq and Conflict Termination: The Road to Guerrilla War?* Washington, DC: Center for Strategic and International Studies.

—— (2003) *Lessons of the Iraq War*. Washington, DC: Center for Strategic and International Studies.

Crane, C. C., and A. W. Terrill (2003) *Reconstructing Iraq: Insights, Challenges, and Missions for Military Forces in a Post-Conflict Scenario*. Carlisle, PA: Strategic Services Institute; <http://www.carlisle.army.mil/ssi/pdffiles/00175.pdf>.

Daponte, B. (1993) 'A Case Study in Estimating Casualties from War and its Aftermath: The 1991 Persian Gulf War', *Medicine and Global Survival*, 3, 2.

Der Derian, J. (2001) *Virtuous War: Mapping the Military–Industrial–Media–Entertainment Network*. Boulder, CO: Westview.

Doorn, J. van (1975) *The Soldier and Social Change*. London: Sage.

Duffield, M. (2001) *Global Governance and the New Wars*. London: Zed.

Edgerton, D. (1991) 'Liberal Militarism and the British State', *New Left Review*, 185, pp. 138–69.

Freedman, L. (1988) *Britain and the Falklands War*. Oxford: Blackwell.

Gamba, V. (1987) *The Falklands-Malvinas War*. Boston: Allen & Unwin.

Garden, T. (2003) 'Iraq: The Military Campaign', *International Affairs*, 79, p. 4.

Giddens, A. (1984) *The Constitution of Society*. Cambridge: Polity.

—— (1985) *The Nation-State and Violence*. Cambridge: Polity.

—— (1990) *The Consequences of Modernity*. Cambridge: Polity.

—— (1991) *Modernity and Self-Identity*. Cambridge: Polity.

Gittlin, T. (2003) 'Globalization, Education and Media: Notes on the Circulation of Media'. Unpublished paper.

Glasgow University Media Group (1985) *War and Peace News*. Milton Keynes: Open University Press.

Gordon, D. (2003) 'Iraq, War and Morality', *Economic and Political Weekly*, 38, pp. 1117–120.

Goulding, V. J., Jr. (2000–1) 'Back to the Future with Asymmetric Warfare', *Parameters*, winter.

Grass, G. (2002) *Crabwalk*. London: Faber & Faber.

Gray, C. S. (1999) *Modern Strategy*. Oxford: Oxford University Press.

—— (2004) *Strategy for Chaos: Revolutions in Military Affairs and the Evidence of History*. London: Cass.

Hallin, D. (1986) *The 'Uncensored War': The Media and Vietnam*. New York: Oxford University Press.

Hammond, P., and E. S. Herman, eds (2000) *Degraded Capability: The Media and the Kosovo Crisis*. London: Pluto.

Hanson, V. D. (1989) *The Western Way of War: Infantry Battle in Classical Greece*. New York: Knopf.

—— (2002) *An Autumn of War: What America Learned from September 11 and the War on Terrorism*. New York: Random House.

—— (2004) *Between War and Peace: Lessons from Afghanistan to Iraq*. New York: Random House.

Heidenrich, J. G. (2003) 'The Gulf War: How Many Iraqis Died?', *Foreign Policy*, 90, 3.

Held, D., A. McGrew, D. Goldblatt and J. Perraton (1999) *Global Transformations*. Cambridge: Polity.

Hobsbawm, E. J. (1993) *The Age of Extremes: The Short Twentieth Century 1914–89*. London: Michael Joseph.

Honig, J. W., and N. Both (1996) *Srebrenica: Record of a War Crime*. London: Penguin.

Howard, M. (1984) *Clausewitz*. Oxford: Oxford University Press.

Human Rights Watch (2003) *Climate of Fear: Sexual Violence and Abduction of Women and Girls in Baghdad*. New York: Human Rights Watch.
—— (2003) *Off Target: The Conduct of the War and Civilian Casualties in Iraq*. New York: Human Rights Watch.
Ignatieff, M. (2001) *Virtual War: Kosovo and Beyond*. London: Vintage.
International Independent Commission on Kosovo (2000) *The Kosovo Report: Conflict, International Response, Lessons Learned*. Oxford: Oxford University Press.
International Institute of Strategic Studies (2000–) *The Military Balance*. Oxford: Oxford University Press [annual].
Joas, H. (2003) *War and Modernity*. Cambridge: Polity.
Kaldor, M. (1982) 'Warfare and Capitalism', in New Left Review, ed., *Exterminism and Cold War*. London: Verso.
—— (1982) *The Baroque Arsenal*. London: Deutsch.
—— (1990) *The Imaginary War*. Oxford: Blackwell.
—— (1999) *New and Old Wars: Organized Violence in a Global Era*. Cambridge: Polity.
—— (2003) 'American Power: From "Compellance" to Cosmopolitanism?', *International Affairs*, 79, 1, pp. 1–22.
—— (2003) *Global Civil Society: An Answer to War*. Cambridge: Polity.
Kaldor, M., and A. Eide, eds (1979) *The World Military Order: The Impact of Military Technology on the Third World*. London: Macmillan.
Kampfner, J. (2003) *Blair's Wars*. London: Free Press.
Kaye, H., and K. McClelland, eds (1990) *E. P. Thompson: Critical Debates*. Cambridge: Polity.
Keaney, T., and E. A. Cohen (1993) *Gulf War Air Power Survey: A Summary*. Washington, DC: Office of the Secretary of the Air Force.
Latham, A. (1999) 'Reimagining Warfare: The "Revolution in Military Affairs"', in C. Snyder, ed., *Contemporary Security and Strategy*. London: Macmillan, pp. 210–37.
Luckham, R. (1984) 'Of Arms and Culture', *Current Research on Peace and Violence*, 7, 1, pp. 1–64.
Luttwak, E. N. (1995) 'Towards Post-Heroic Warfare', *Foreign Affairs*, 74, 3.
McInnes, C., and G. D. Sheffield, eds (1988) *Warfare in the Twentieth Century: Theory and Practice*. London: Unwin Hyman.
MacNeill, W. H. (1982) *The Pursuit of Power*. Oxford: Blackwell.
Makiya, K. (1993) *Cruelty and Silence: War, Tyranny, Uprising, and the Arab World*. London: Cape.
Mandelbaum, M. (1987) 'Vietnam: The Television War', *Daedalus*, 3, 4, pp. 157–69.
Mann, M. (1986, 1993) *The Sources of Social Power*, vols 1 and 2. Cambridge: Cambridge University Press.

—— (1987) 'The Roots and Contradictions of Modern Militarism', *New Left Review*, 162.

—— (1988) *States, War and Capitalism*. Oxford: Blackwell.

—— (2003) *Incoherent Empire*. London: Verso.

Marwick, A., ed. (1988) *Total War and Social Change*. Basingstoke: Macmillan.

Mathews, J., and J. Cirincione (2003) 'Q & A on Iraq's Weapons Programs', *Proliferation Brief* [Carnegie Endowment for International Peace], 6, 14; <http://www.ceip.org/files/nonprolif/templates/Publications.asp?p=8&PublicationID=1327>.

Melvern, L. (2000) *A People Betrayed: The Role of the West in Rwanda's Genocide*. London: Zed.

Middle East Watch (1993) *Genocide in Iraq: The Anfal Campaign Against the Kurds*. New York: Human Rights Watch.

Miller, D., ed. (2003) *Tell Me Lies: Propaganda and Media Distortion in the Attack on Iraq*. London: Pluto.

Monaghan, D. (1998) *The Falklands War: Myth and Countermyth*. Basingstoke: Macmillan.

Morrison, D., and H. Tumber (1988) *Journalists at War: The Dynamics of News Reporting during the Falklands Conflict*. London: Sage.

Moskos, C., and F. Wood, eds (1988) *The Military: More Than Just a Job?* Oxford: Pergamon-Brassey.

Moskos, C., J. Williams and D. Segal, eds (2000) *The Postmodern Military: Armed Forces after the Cold War*. New York: Oxford University Press.

Murphy, M., and C. Conetta, eds (2003) *Civilian Casualties in the 2003 Iraq War: A Compendium of Accounts and Reports*. Cambridge, MA: Project on Defense Alternatives.

Murray, W., and R. H. Scales (2003) *The Iraq War: A Military History*. Cambridge, MA: Belknap Press.

Nacos, B. L. (2002) *Mass-Mediated Terrorism: The Central Role of the Media in Terrorism and Counter-Terrorism*. Lanham, MD: Rowman & Littlefield.

O'Hanlon, M. (2002) 'A Flawed Masterpiece', *Foreign Affairs*, 81, p. 3.

Pollack, K. (2002) *Threatening Storm: The Case for Invading Iraq*. New York: Random House.

Power, S. (2003) *'A Problem from Hell': America and the Age of Genocide*. London: Flamingo.

Rai, M. (2003) *Regime Unchanged: Why the War on Iraq Changed Nothing*. London: Pluto.

Rieff, D. (1995) *Slaughterhouse: Bosnia and the Failure of the West*. London: Vintage.

Rizer, K. (2001) 'Bombing Dual-Use Targets: Legal, Ethical, and Doctrinal Perspectives', *Air and Space Power Chronicles*, <http://www.airpower.maxwell.af.mil/airchronicles/cc/Rizer.html> [10 September 2003].

Roberts, A., and R. Guelff, eds (2000) *Documents on the Laws of War*. Oxford: Oxford University Press.

Robertson, L. R. (2004) *The Dream of Civilized Warfare: World War I Flying Aces and the American Imagination*. Minneapolis: University of Minnesota Press.

Rutherford, P. (2004) *Weapons of Mass Persuasion: Marketing the War against Iraq*. Toronto and London: University of Toronto Press.

Schabas, W. (2000) *Genocide in International Law*. Cambridge: Cambridge University Press.

Scott, A. (2000) 'Risk Society or Angst Society?', in B. Adam, U. Beck and J. van Loon, eds, *Risk Society and Beyond*. London: Sage, pp. 33–45.

Shaw, M. (1988) *Dialectics of War*. London: Pluto.

—— (1991) *Post-Military Society*. Cambridge: Polity.

—— (1994) *Global Society and International Relations*. Cambridge: Polity.

—— (1996) *Civil Society and Media in Global Crises*. London: Pinter.

—— (2000) 'The Contemporary Mode of Warfare? Mary Kaldor's Theory of New Wars', *Review of International Political Economy*, 7, 1, pp. 171–80.

—— (2000) *Theory of the Global State*. Cambridge: Cambridge University Press.

—— (2002) 'Risk-Transfer Militarism, Small Massacres and the Historic Legitimacy of War', *International Relations*, 16, 3, pp. 343–60.

—— (2003) *War and Genocide*. Cambridge: Polity.

Shaw, M., and Carr-Hill, R. (1991) *Public Opinion, Media and Violence: Attitudes to the Gulf War in a Local Population*. Hull: Hull University Gulf War Project.

Slim, H. (2003) 'Why Protect Civilians? Innocence, Immunity and Enmity in War', *International Affairs*, 79, 3, pp. 481–501.

Small, M., and J. D. Singer (1982) *Resort to Arms: International and Civil Wars 1816–1980*. London: Sage.

Smith, D., with A. Bræin (2003) *The Atlas of War and Peace*. 4th edn, London: Earthscan.

Smith, M. L. R. (2003) 'Guerrillas in the Mist: Reassessing Strategy and Low Intensity Warfare', *Review of International Studies*, 29, pp. 19–37.

Snyder, C. A., ed. (1999) *Contemporary Security and Strategy*. London: Macmillan.

Taylor, P. (1992) *War and the Media: Propaganda and Persuasion in the Gulf War*. Manchester: Manchester University Press.

Thompson, E. P. (1982) 'Exterminism: The Last Stage of Civilisation', in New Left Review, ed., *Exterminism and Cold War*. London: Verso, pp. 1–34.

Todd, E. (2002) *After the Empire: The Breakdown of the American Order*. New York: Columbia University Press.

Tumber, H., and J. Palmer (2004) *Media at War: The Iraq Crisis*. London: Sage.

UK Government (2002) 'Iraq's Weapons of Mass Destruction – The Assessment of the British Government', <http://www.number-10.gov.uk/output/Page271.asp>.

Von Hippel, K. (1999) *Democracy by Force*. Cambridge: Cambridge University Press.

Walzer, M. (1992) *Just and Unjust Wars*. 2nd edn, New York: Basic Books.

Weber, M. (1947) *The Theory of Social and Economic Organization*. Glencoe, IL: Free Press.

Weissman, F., ed. (2004) *In the Shadow of 'Just Wars': Violence, Politics and Humanitarian Action*. London: Hurst.

Wheeler, N. J. (2000) *Saving Strangers*. Oxford: Oxford University Press.

—— (2002) 'Dying for Enduring Freedom: Accepting Responsibility for Casualties in the War Against Terrorism', *International Relations*, 16, 2, pp. 105–25.

Index